ID0604853

Praise for *Worry-Free Investing*

"With this book, Bodie and Clowes have made a very valuable contribution to an area which has been attracting increasing attention in recent years, that of accumulating the proper amount of resources for future goals and, in particular, for an adequate retirement. It is a subject very close to my heart as I have devoted to it much of my professional effort, and it has earned me a Nobel Prize. What is special about this book is its emphasis on safety. When I was writing about retirement saving some 50 years ago, I made an heroic assumption that people could carry resources into the future in a reliably safe way; at that time it was an unrealistic assumption. But as the authors delight in showing, over the last 50 years things have changed enormously. So they can not only emphasize the importance of safety first but are in a position to point to the instruments now existing to implement such a policy. This book is a must for those timid souls who don't enjoy risk taking . . . like me."

—Franco Modigliani, Nobel Prize Winner, Economics

"The arrival of *Worry-Free Investing* with its sage advice on investing for our most important financial goals could not have been better timed. The large decline in world stock markets in these last three years have left many of us with a pressing need to reassess our investment strategy for financing our retirement and to reconsider how much risk we are really willing to tolerate. Bodie and Clowes are uniquely qualified to help us with this task, combining a world-class scholarly research background with extensive real-world experience in advising financial institutions, corporations, and sovereigns on the subject of retirement finance. The talented and experienced team of authors both explains the key pitfalls in commonly offered advice on retirement investing and constructively suggests an innovative alternative approach. Their plain-spoken analysis and prescriptions for action are focused on realistic evaluations of what it takes to achieve financial goals with minimal risk, including how to get the most out of the assets you have. Despite the sophisticated financial thinking underlying its recommendations, this book is accessible to all. Indeed, a likely reaction is that it just seems like good common sense. Perhaps. But it's a common sense that the reader will be hard-pressed to find in other books of this type or in Internet-based financial advice engines. As promised by its title, the focus of this book is on investment safety. But it is also a good read for those who are prepared to take significant investment risks: Creating a strong financial foundation to ensure essential goals predicates any strategy of intelligent and sustainable risk taking."

—Robert C. Merton, Harvard University, Nobel Prize Winner, Economics

"A provocative and powerful debunking of the sovereign myth of equities as the *camino real* to retirement adequacy. This lucid and assuring guide is like none other in answering the individual investor's call for practical, trustworthy advice for safely achieving financial security. Highly recommended."

—Alan Cleveland, of Counsel to Sheehan Phinney, Bass and Green

"Bodie and Clowes' book is a useful compass for navigating the uncertain and sometimes treacherous waters of investing. Their insights deliver results."

—Louis Columbus, Senior Analyst, AMR Research

"*Worry-Free Investing* will enable you to achieve your retirement plans no matter what the stock and bond markets are doing. Bodie and Clowes present a safe way to build and control wealth. The methods are thoroughly and simply explained. Yet, the ideas stem from rigorous research and state-of-the-art science. This book is just what millions of investors need in these tough times."

—John R. Nofsinger, Finance professor, Washington State University, author of *Investment Madness*, *Investment Blunder*, and *Infectious Greed*

"Bodie and Clowes' book is the most timely personal finance book of the year. Retirement investors, severely affected by the dot-com market bubble and employer's 401(k) malfeasance, are given simple ideas that will restore their hope in planning for retirement. It is a clarion call for 401(k) innovation and adding choices for TIPS (Treasury) bonds and equity funds containing downside protection. Such sensible, powerful retirement advice is truly a public service. Both authors deserve the Pulitzer Prize!"

—Clinton E. Day, Chartered Retirement Planning Counselor

"Zvi Bodie and Michael Clowes have presented the proverbial 'missing link' to reliable investment management and worry-free financial planning. Considering the thousands of books available on equity investing, there is a remarkable shortage of information on risk-free bond and alternative income asset classes. This unique book will single-handedly help you balance your knowledge base as well as your portfolio.

"Uncomplicated and unbiased, this is a must read for everyone who needs to provide themselves with a sustainable income throughout their retirement. You won't find this material in any other investment book, when you are done lend your copy to a Financial Planner."

—Barry Cook, *Do-It-Yourself Investor*

Worry-Free Investing

A Safe Approach to Achieving Your Lifetime Financial Goals

In an increasingly competitive world, it is quality
of thinking that gives an edge—an idea that opens new
doors, a technique that solves a problem, or an insight
that simply helps make sense of it all.

We work with leading authors in the various arenas
of business and finance to bring cutting-edge thinking
and best learning practice to a global market.

It is our goal to create world-class print publications
and electronic products that give readers
knowledge and understanding which can then be
applied, whether studying or at work.

To find out more about our business
products, you can visit us at www.ft-ph.com

Worry-Free Investing

A Safe Approach to Achieving Your Lifetime Financial Goals

Zvi Bodie

Michael J. Clowes

FT Prentice Hall

FINANCIAL TIMES

An Imprint of PEARSON EDUCATION
Upper Saddle River, NJ • New York • London • San Francisco • Toronto • Sydney
Tokyo • Singapore • Hong Kong • Cape Town • Madrid
Paris • Milan • Munich • Amsterdam

www.ft-ph.com

Library of Congress Cataloging-in Publication Data

Bodie, Zvi
  Worry-free investing : a safe approach to achieving your lifetime financial goals/ by Zvi
Bodie and Michael Clowes.
    p. cm.
Includes bibliographic references and index.
ISBN 0-13-049927-7
  1. Investments--United States. 2. Inflation-indexed bonds--United States. 3.
Stocks--United States. 4. Finance, Personal--United States. I. Clowes, Michael J., 1942–
II. Title.

HG4910.B597 2003
332.6--dc21   2003040888

Editor-in-Chief: *Timothy C. Moore*
Editorial/Production Supervision: *Donna Cullen-Dolce*
Development Editor: *Russ Hall*
Manufacturing Manager: *Alexis R. Heydt-Long*
Manufacturing Buyer: *Maura Zaldivar*
Interior Design: *Gail Cocker-Bogusz*
Cover Design Director: *Jerry Votta*
Cover Design: *Talar Boorujy*

© 2003 by Pearson Education, Inc.
Publishing as Financial Times Prentice Hall
Upper Saddle River, New Jersey 07458

Financial Times Prentice Hall offers excellent discounts on this book when ordered in quantity for bulk purchases or special sales. For more information, please contact U.S. Corporate and Government Sales: 1- 800-382-3419, or corpsales@pearsontechgroup.com. For sales outside the United States, please contact International Sales: 1-317-581-3793, international@pearsonetechgroup.com

Any company and product names mentioned herein are the trademarks or registered trademarks of their respective owners.

All rights reserved. No part of this book may be reproduced, in any form or by any means, without permission in writing from the publisher.

Printed in the United States of America
1st Printing

ISBN 0-13-049927-7

Pearson Education LTD.
Pearson Education Australia PTY, Limited
Pearson Education Singapore, Pte. Ltd.
Pearson Education North Asia Ltd.
Pearson Education Canada, Ltd.
Pearson Educación de Mexico, S.A. de C.V.
Pearson Education—Japan
Pearson Education Malaysia, Pte. Ltd.

FINANCIAL TIMES PRENTICE HALL BOOKS

For more information, please go to www.ft-ph.com

Business and Technology
Sarv Devaraj and Rajiv Kohli
> *The IT Payoff: Measuring the Business Value of Information Technology Investments*

Nicholas D. Evans
> *Business Agility: Strategies for Gaining Competitive Advantage through Mobile Business Solutions*

Nicholas D. Evans
> *Business Innovation and Disruptive Technology: Harnessing the Power of Breakthrough Technology...for Competitive Advantage*

Nicholas D. Evans
> *Consumer Gadgets: 50 Ways to Have Fun and Simplify Your Life with Today's Technology...and Tomorrow's*

Faisal Hoque
> *The Alignment Effect: How to Get Real Business Value Out of Technology*

Thomas Kern, Mary Cecelia Lacity, and Leslie P. Willcocks
> *Netsourcing: Renting Business Applications and Services Over a Network*

Ecommerce
Dale Neef
> *E-procurement: From Strategy to Implementation*

Economics
David Dranove
> *What's Your Life Worth? Health Care Rationing...Who Lives? Who Dies? Who Decides?*

David R. Henderson
> *The Joy of Freedom: An Economist's Odyssey*

Jonathan Wight
> *Saving Adam Smith: A Tale of Wealth, Transformation, and Virtue*

Entrepreneurship
Oren Fuerst and Uri Geiger
> *From Concept to Wall Street: A Complete Guide to Entrepreneurship and Venture Capital*

David Gladstone and Laura Gladstone
> *Venture Capital Handbook: An Entrepreneur's Guide to Raising Venture Capital, Revised and Updated*

Erica Orloff and Kathy Levinson, Ph.D.
> *The 60-Second Commute: A Guide to Your 24/7 Home Office Life*

Jeff Saperstein and Daniel Rouach
> *Creating Regional Wealth in the Innovation Economy: Models, Perspectives, and Best Practices*

Finance

Aswath Damodaran
  *The Dark Side of Valuation: Valuing Old Tech, New Tech, and New
  Economy Companies*
Kenneth R. Ferris and Barbara S. Pécherot Petitt
  Valuation: Avoiding the Winner's Curse

International Business

Peter Marber
  *Money Changes Everything: How Global Prosperity Is Reshaping Our Needs,
  Values, and Lifestyles*
Fernando Robles, Françoise Simon, and Jerry Haar
  Winning Strategies for the New Latin Markets

Investments

Zvi Bodie and Michael J. Clowes
  Worry-Free Investing: A Safe Approach to Achieving Your Lifetime Goals
Harry Domash
  Fire Your Stock Analyst! Analyzing Stocks on Your Own
Philip Jenks and Stephen Eckett, Editors
  *The Global-Investor Book of Investing Rules: Invaluable Advice from 150
  Master Investors*
Charles P. Jones
  *Mutual Funds: Your Money, Your Choice. Take Control Now and Build
  Wealth Wisely*
D. Quinn Mills
  Buy, Lie, and Sell High: How Investors Lost Out on Enron and the Internet Bubble
D. Quinn Mills
  *Wheel, Deal, and Steal: Deceptive Accounting, Deceitful CEOs, and Ineffective
  Reforms*
John Nofsinger and Kenneth Kim
  Infectious Greed: Restoring Confidence in America's Companies
John R. Nofsinger
  Investment Blunders (of the Rich and Famous)…And What You Can Learn from Them
John R. Nofsinger
  *Investment Madness: How Psychology Affects Your Investing…And What to Do
  About It*

Leadership

Jim Despain and Jane Bodman Converse
  And Dignity for All: Unlocking Greatness through Values-Based Leadership
Marshall Goldsmith, Vijay Govindarajan, Beverly Kaye, and Albert A. Vicere
  The Many Facets of Leadership
Marshall Goldsmith, Cathy Greenberg, Alastair Robertson, and Maya Hu-Chan
  Global Leadership: The Next Generation

Frederick C. Militello, Jr., and Michael D. Schwalberg
Leverage Competencies: What Financial Executives Need to Lead
Eric G. Stephan and Wayne R. Pace
Powerful Leadership: How to Unleash the Potential in Others and Simplify Your Own Life

Management

Rob Austin and Lee Devin
Artful Making: What Managers Need to Know About How Artists Work
Dr. Judith M. Bardwick
Seeking the Calm in the Storm: Managing Chaos in Your Business Life
J. Stewart Black and Hal B. Gregersen
Leading Strategic Change: Breaking Through the Brain Barrier
William C. Byham, Audrey B. Smith, and Matthew J. Paese
Grow Your Own Leaders: How to Identify, Develop, and Retain Leadership Talent
David M. Carter and Darren Rovell
On the Ball: What You Can Learn About Business from Sports Leaders
Subir Chowdhury
Organization 21C: Someday All Organizations Will Lead this Way
Subir Chowdhury
The Talent Era: Achieving a High Return on Talent
James W. Cortada
Making the Information Society: Experience, Consequences, and Possibilities
Ross Dawson
Living Networks: Leading Your Company, Customers, and Partners in the Hyper-connected Economy
Robert B. Handfield, Ph.d, and Ernest L. Nichols
Supply Chain Redesign: Transforming Supply Chains into Integrated Value Systems
Harvey A. Hornstein
The Haves and the Have Nots: The Abuse of Power and Privilege in the Workplace... and How to Control It
Kevin Kennedy and Mary Moore
Going the Distance: Why Some Companies Dominate and Others Fail
Robin Miller
The Online Rules of Successful Companies: The Fool-Proof Guide to Building Profits
Fergus O'Connell
The Competitive Advantage of Common Sense: Using the Power You Already Have
Richard W. Paul and Linda Elder
Critical Thinking: Tools for Taking Charge of Your Professional and Personal Life
Matthew Serbin Pittinsky, Editor
The Wired Tower: Perspectives on the Impact of the Internet on Higher Education

W. Alan Randolph and Barry Z. Posner
Checkered Flag Projects: 10 Rules for Creating and Managing Projects that Win, Second Edition

Stephen P. Robbins
The Truth About Managing People…And Nothing but the Truth

Ronald Snee and Roger Hoerl
Leading Six Sigma: A Step-by-Step Guide Based on Experience with GE and Other Six Sigma Companies

Jerry Weissman
Presenting to Win: The Art of Telling Your Story

Marketing

Michael Basch
CustomerCulture: How FedEx and Other Great Companies Put the Customer First Every Day

Deirdre Breakenridge
Cyberbranding: Brand Building in the Digital Economy

Jonathan Cagan and Craig M. Vogel
Creating Breakthrough Products: Innovation from Product Planning to Program Approval

James W. Cortada
21st Century Business: Managing and Working in the New Digital Economy

Al Lieberman, with Patricia Esgate
The Entertainment Marketing Revolution: Bringing the Moguls, the Media, and the Magic to the World

Tom Osenton
Customer Share Marketing: How the World's Great Marketers Unlock Profits from Customer Loyalty

Yoram J. Wind and Vijay Mahajan, with Robert Gunther
Convergence Marketing: Strategies for Reaching the New Hybrid Consumer

Public Relations

Gerald R. Baron
Now Is Too Late: Survival in an Era of Instant News

Deirdre Breakenridge and Thomas J. DeLoughry
The New PR Toolkit: Strategies for Successful Media Relations

Strategy

Thomas L. Barton, William G. Shenkir, and Paul L. Walker
Making Enterprise Risk Management Pay Off: How Leading Companies Implement Risk Management

Henry A. Davis and William W. Sihler
Financial Turnarounds: Preserving Enterprise Value

I dedicate this book to my friend, Robert C. Merton, who taught me finance, and to my wife, Judy Bodie, who taught me the meaning of love.

—ZB

To Ellen, John Paul, Molly, and Jeffrey

—MJC

C · O · N · T · E · N · T · S

Planning your own financial investments can be complex. Let no one make a mistake about that. Such planning can be made more stressful by uncertain times. You may have witnessed your own stock portfolio and the portfolios of friends diminishing significantly in value, even largely diversified ones. You may have seen your company 401(k) reports taking many steps backward instead of forward. Money put in, and matched by the company, has dwindled even since being deposited. Employees at companies like Enron have had an even more shocking experience.

Aside from the volatility of the stock market, there are the traditional concerns for investment—whether you're saving toward your retirement or your children's education—inflation, taxes, even the cost of investing. Savings accounts, CDs, and traditional bonds don't generate what they once did. Social Security is neither sure nor sufficient. What do you do about all of these?

On top of all of this, there is change. Everything you know, or can know, is subject to ever-constant change. How can you keep up with all you need to know toward the most worry-free path to investment? That is the mission of this book, and it has the right men for the job, ones who closely follow the pulse of change.

The authors are experts with years of experience in investment research, education, and consulting. **Zvi Bodie** is a professor of finance and a consultant in the investments field. His textbooks

Investments and *Finance* (Prentice Hall) have been translated into 10 languages and are used at the top business schools around the world. **Michael J. Clowes** is Editorial Director of *Pensions and Investments* and *Investment News*. His most recent book is *The Money Flood* (John Wiley & Sons).

Zvi Bodie and Mike Clowes have closely followed the changes in the financial investment scene, and they mean to turn this to your ultimate advantage, and do so in clear steps. Using the situations of people like you, they cut through the clutter of what may seem the chaos of change. They share their insights on what has changed to your advantage. They want you to understand and be able to implement strategies that work for your busy life, suited to your specific needs.

You don't have the time to become a professional investor; you have a full-time job already. What you want are some simple and easy steps that you can use to ensure that your investments will be there when you want them to be.

In the most simple terms, the first 10 chapters of *Worry-Free Investing* present the bare minimum of what you need to know: what the changes in the financial scene are, how you can use them to your advantage, and the steps you need to take to more worry-free investing. By the time you have read these forthright and informative chapters, you should know everything you need to make good financial decisions on which you can bank.

Foreword

The remaining chapters provide you with further food for thought if you wish to delve a bit deeper into the basic strategies espoused here: responses to frequently asked questions; more detailed guidance on evaluating your financial risk now; a guide to managing your finances when you do retire; plus, some terrific Internet resources you can use to become even more informed.

It is normal to worry, especially about something as important as your retirement, your children's college fund, or some other important goal in times when the traditional vehicles of investment falter and fail.

There are ways to reduce your financial risk, and with it your worry. There may be no panacea, no pill that instantly fixes everything, but *Worry-Free Investing* goes a long way toward easing your mind by clearly informing you on exactly how to address your financial needs, to customize your investments so that they are tailored to that need, and to implement a more worry-free program—whether you handle your own investments or use what you learn here to speak with your financial advisor in a more informed way.

I have read this book as avidly as I hope you will. We all are looking for the same kind of answers. I believe Zvi Bodie and Mike Clowes address those answers as well as anyone in the investment scene at the moment. Read *Worry-Free Investing*, consider what it has to say, and, for heaven's sake, worry a bit less.

—Timothy C. Moore,
Editor-in-Chief,
Financial Times Prentice Hall

P ··· R ··· E ··· F ··· A ··· C ··· E ················

The past few years have shocked and dismayed investors who had been relying on the stock market to pay for their future goals. After 20 years of almost uninterrupted gains, stock prices have declined sharply. Millions of Americans who had believed the mantra that stocks are unbeatable in the long run are now worried about achieving their retirement goals and their hopes of paying college tuition for their children.

Are you one of these worried investors? If so, this book is for you. In these pages you will learn that:

· There is a safe, worry-free way to beat inflation—invest in Consumer Price Index (CPI) linked bonds. In April 1997, the U.S. Treasury began issuing these bonds, which protect investors against increases in the cost of living for up to 30 years. In 1998, the Treasury introduced convenient tax-advantaged CPI-linked saving bonds in denominations as small as $50. The Treasury's stated intention was to encourage personal saving by providing a safe way to invest money for retirement and other long-term goals. Yet today, only a few years after they came into existence, many Americans are not even aware that such securities exist. We provide step-by-step instructions for using them to safely achieve your financial goals.

· There are ways to invest in inflation-protected retirement-income contracts that are guaranteed to last for as long as you live.

- There is a worry-free way to invest your savings for a child's college tuition—buy tuition-linked Certificates of Deposit (CDs). These tax-advantaged, government-insured accounts are even safer than CPI-linked bonds, although they promise a lower rate of interest.

- Buying your own home may be your biggest investment. We show how to use your own home as a means to invest safely for retirement and to pay for your living expenses in old age.

- If you are willing to accept the risk of losing some of your money, there are sensible ways to increase your potential gains by investing in stocks, or in mutual funds, or in related securities, such as Exchange-Traded Funds (ETFs). We help you decide if you can afford to take such risk and provide step-by-step instructions for doing so without paying large fees to brokers and money managers.

- Stocks are not safe in the long run. Stocks offer the potential for large gains, but they expose you to the risk of large losses. This is true even when your stock portfolio is well diversified across different companies and industries. Don't believe those who try to convince you that the risk goes away if you hold stocks for more than 5, 10, or even 30 years. This is wishful thinking.

Inside these pages, you make some important evaluations and ask yourself the most important question of all in relation to investment and risk, which is, **"How much can I afford to**

lose?" With that in mind, you will consider several ways to substantially reduce your risk to its lowest possible level. The objective, by the end of this book, is for you to understand and implement a plan for worry-free investing.

The simple formula that governs this entire approach is for you to know and use ways to invest that take less chances—ones that are backed by guarantees or that hedge the taking of chances. Why is this important to you? Because investing in ways that take chances (whether in the stock market, 401(k) plans, or mutual funds) can make great gains, but can as readily make great losses (as we all have witnessed). The only way to eliminate worry is to eliminate risk. If making consistent investment gains with as little worry as possible is your objective, then this is the book for you.

Acknowledgments

We thank our editor, Tim Moore, for motivating us to write this book and for working with us tirelessly to get it done. We thank Russ Hall for helping to make it understandable and fun to read. If any part of this book is dull, inaccurate, or inscrutable, the blame rests entirely on us.

—Zvi Bodie and Michael J. Clowes

Worry-Free Investing

1

New Rules for Investing

In this chapter, you explore:

· What has gone horribly wrong with investing

· A new strategy based on new investment vehicles

· Six Steps to Worry-Free Investing

The conventional wisdom about investing says that a diversified portfolio of stocks is not risky in the long run. The conventional wisdom is wrong! It has caused much grief and pain to millions of investors, who have lost billions of dollars because they have relied on that advice.

Take the case of John and Joan Parker, people very much like you, who in March 2000 were looking forward to retirement in two years. **John, a marketing executive, would be 62 at the**

end of 2002. If the stock market gave just 10% per year for those years, John would have enough, with early Social Security, for a comfortable retirement income of more than $90,000 a year for himself and Joan.

That would have been enough for them to move from their two-story, four-bedroom, long-paid-for Trenton, New Jersey, home to a new, less-expensive two-bedroom house with lower property taxes on the outskirts of Greenville, North Carolina. There John could easily drive to either the Bradford Golf Club or the Lee Trevino signature Ironwood Golf Course. Not that John had done more than gather stacks of pamphlets and fly down to play the courses twice (he'd even taken a few lessons to lower his handicap by three strokes and was eyeing a new set of titanium clubs). Joan had already picked out an affordable home that looked ideal (she was gathering swatches of cloth samples and having long talks with a friend who'd once been an interior designer).

With the two kids grown and gone—John, Jr., self-sufficient after getting his MBA and a position with a Fortune 500 company, and Caroline, just graduated with a computer engineering degree and a good job in the Seattle area—they no longer needed the bigger house. It seemed like a good time to start over for the senior Parkers, in a location where food prices were a bit lower and the climate was milder.

Early retirement looked like a sure thing. John's 401(k) was 80% in stock mutual funds, and the market was going gangbusters, as it had for the previous several years. John was a bit concerned because he knew some financial advisors said he should already have reduced his exposure to the stock market. A popular rule he kept hearing was that the proportion in stocks should be equal to 100 minus your age. In John's case that meant 40%. In the end, John decided to stay in the market because everyone he knew was racking up big gains. Stock experts on television were saying the economy had been changed by technology and the market could continue climbing indefinitely. He knew he would feel foolish if he took his money out and watched while everyone else was making big gains. **John decided to wait until he retired to make any changes in his asset mix. That was a bad decision.**

By March 2002, the stock market collapse had changed the Parkers' world. Their retirement portfolio was worth only half the sum they had projected. John and Joan took a long hard look at their financial picture, considered every step open to them, even to selling Joan's lifelong stamp collection on eBay. John cancelled his session with his golf pro scheduled for that weekend, and Joan quietly packed up her sample swatches of materials. **John's mouth settled into a firm line as he reluctantly faced the fact that he would have to work a few more years. Joan went off to another room to be alone.** The freshly decorated cozy new home in North Carolina moved farther away for Joan, and those imagined sunny days on the golf courses would have to wait for John.

But it could have been worse. At least the Parkers were relatively well diversified. Bob and Sandy Adams, of Toledo, Ohio, believed they had their son Chuck's college tuition all taken care of through a mutual fund account invested in growth stocks. Instead, they saw their college fund fall by 80%. Suddenly, Chuck's dream of going to Princeton was about to shift to Ohio State. Even with a student loan, Princeton's tuition looked out of reach now.

Don't forget about already-retired Betty Sue Hampton, former Enron employee in Houston, Texas, whose entire 401(k) was in company stock. She saw her entire retirement fund disappear in a cloud of scandalous dust. A widow, she had to sell her beloved lifelong home and move into an apartment complex.

This was not the first time that an uncooperative stock market had upset people's retirement plans. Back in 1973, the picture would have been even more difficult for John and Joan Parker. With 100% invested in stocks, they would have lost half of their retirement savings over the two years 1973 and 1974. (See Figure 1.1.) In addition, the high inflation of those years would have eroded the purchasing power of what remained. That would have been true whether it was invested in stocks or conventional bonds.

As it was, the Parkers decided that after the results of 2000 and 2001 (see Figure 1.2), they would not only save more for a few extra years, they would reconsider their whole approach to investing. They were determined to find an investment strategy that would not force them to change their retirement plans again.

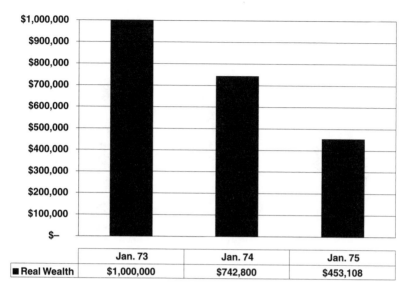

	Jan. 73	Jan. 74	Jan. 75
■ Real Wealth	$1,000,000	$742,800	$453,108

Figure 1.1
Shrinkage of real value of $1 million invested in the stock
market in 1973–74.

They wanted the assurance that once retired they would not have
to take part-time employment to make ends meet.

A New Strategy

**There is a strategy, and this book explains it to you. It
is guaranteed to succeed even in the worst bear
market. You will see how to achieve your goals—a
comfortable retirement, a child's college education,
or even a cruise around the world—with far lower
risk. You'll get step-by-step instructions on how to
invest enough in inflation-protected bonds and other**

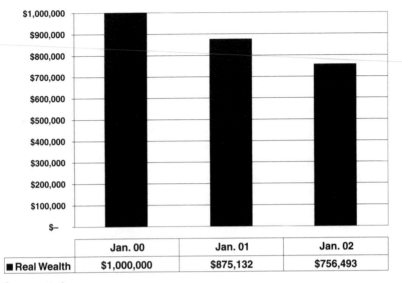

	Jan. 00	Jan. 01	Jan. 02
■ Real Wealth	$1,000,000	$875,132	$756,493

Figure 1.2
Shrinkage of real value of $1 million invested in the stock market in 2000–2001.

risk-free investments to reach your goals exactly when you have planned.

If you want to sleep nights secure in the knowledge that you will achieve your savings goal, you must invest in a way that eliminates the possibility that inflation will undercut your efforts. If you try to do it by saving less and expecting the stock market to do the heavy lifting, you may not get there at all. Relying on the stock market to provide a major part of your retirement income is relying on chance—like the rolling of the dice. The odds are better in the stock market, but it's still risky.

Bad Advice

John and Joan Parker, Bob and Sandy Adams, and millions of investors like them, were victims of the conventional wisdom—and that was based on dangerous misinformation. They were taking big risks of which they were totally unaware. They and multitudes of others were expecting the stock market to give them so much return that they could afford a comfortable retirement without having to really tighten their belts to save. They took the risk because the experts told them that if you diversify your portfolio across stocks of many different companies and hold those stocks long enough, there is little risk. The experts also said that the only way to earn a real return on your investments—a return greater than the rate of inflation—was to invest in the stock market. All of this was the conventional wisdom—and still is.

Bob and Sandy Adams plunged into stocks to build Chuck's college fund, attracted by the high returns the stock market had provided over the previous 15 years and reassured by those experts that said if they held stocks long enough they would not be risky. In fact, some experts argued stocks were *less* risky than bonds. Those experts were right if the comparison was with conventional bonds, but dead wrong if the comparison is with the new inflation-indexed bonds issued by the U.S. Treasury.

Conventional wisdom is wrong. Stocks don't always produce the highest return, diversification doesn't always protect you against loss, and the risk of owning stocks does not always decline the longer you

hold them. Stocks are risky, and remain risky, no matter how long you own them.

Until 1997, investors had little alternative because there was no risk-free way to earn a decent real rate of return that would not be eroded by inflation. Ordinary bonds were chewed up by inflation during the 1970s, so they weren't an alternative to stocks for those saving for retirement or to put a child through college. Real estate generally performed well during the 1970s, but then it got clobbered during the 1980s as well.

In 1997, the U.S. government introduced inflation-indexed bonds—and these have changed all the rules. Unfortunately, most people have never heard of inflation-indexed bonds, and very few of those who have realize their implications.

Because these new bonds and other inflation-protected invest-ments have come along, you can invest *without worry*. You can use them to safely achieve your goal of paying for a child's college education or your own retirement. **You can be certain of the amount your investments will return, no matter what the rate of inflation before and during your retire-ment, and no matter what happens to the stock market.**

Most important, these new investments aren't difficult to under-stand or buy.

New Investments

Inflation-indexed bonds come in two varieties, I Bonds and Treasury Inflation-Protected Securities (TIPS). While they do basically the same job, there are significant tax differences. All investors should invest at least some of their retirement money in these inflation-indexed bonds. **We believe employers should make them available to employees within 401(k) and other voluntary tax-advantaged plans.**

There are circumstances when you will want to take calculated risks by investing in the stock market in the hope of increasing your future income or wealth. We will discuss these circumstances in later chapters. But if you want to hit specific targets for certain, then worry-free investing with inflation-protected securities is the way to go.

Six Steps to Worry-Free Investing

The essence of this book's worry-free investment approach can be summed up in the following six-step process:

1. **Set goals.** Make a list of the specific goals you want to achieve through your saving and investment plan. For example, "I want to continue to live at my customary standard of living after I retire," or "I want to pay for my children's college tuition at Harvard."

2. **Specify targets.** Determine the amount of money you will need to achieve each goal. These amounts become the

targets of your plan. The very definition of risky or safe investing will depend on the target. TIPS and I Bonds have substantially lowered risk if the goal is retirement, but for college saving, special tuition-linked accounts are safer.

3. **Compute your required no-risk saving rate.** Figure out how much you need to save as a fraction of your earnings on the assumption that you take no investment risk. For many people, it is appropriate to count your house as a retirement asset.

4. **Determine your tolerance for risk.** Using as your benchmark the lowered-risk plan you have created in Steps 1–3, evaluate how much risk you are willing to take. Your capacity to tolerate investment risk should be related to the riskiness of your projected future earnings and your ability and willingness to postpone retirement if necessary. The safer your job and your future earnings, the greater your tolerance for risk in your investments. The more willing you are to postpone retirement if your risky investments perform badly, the greater your tolerance for risk.

5. **Choose your risky asset portfolio.** After deciding how much of your wealth you are willing to put at risk, choose a form for taking the risk that gives you the greatest expected gain in welfare.

6. **Minimize taxes and transaction costs.** Make sure that you are not paying any more in taxes, fees, or other investment costs than is necessary.

You have been reacquainted with what now may seem the obvious uncertainty of investment (though this was less obvious in those heady bull market times). You looked at ways to deal with inflation and reduce risk. You briefly considered Six Steps to Worry-Free Investing that you should use when considering your investments. We will develop these steps further throughout the book.

In the following chapters, you get all of the information you need to understand and accomplish each of the steps outlined above. In Chapter 9, we pull it all together for you in an easy-to-understand action plan that you can implement right away or bring to a professional advisor for review before taking action.

For now, take a look in Chapter 2 at how you can lower your risk and costs of investing.

2

Investing with Inflation-Protected Bonds

In this chapter, you explore:

· How to calculate the amount you should invest to reach your specific goal

· How I Bonds enable you to beat inflation

· How to choose between I Bonds and Treasury Inflation-Protected Securities (TIPS)

Setting Clear Goals

You probably have some idea of what your investment goals are, though you may not have worked out specific details like exact amounts needed. At the very least, you know that you should save and invest for the future. But have you fixed on a goal and thought out exactly the steps needed to reach it?

There are some financial goals that are so important to your future welfare that you want to be sure you score a bull's-eye.

Arguably, the two most important goals are:

1. Achieving a minimum acceptable retirement income
2. Paying for a child's education

You may also wish to travel, leave a bequest for your family, or even buy a special treat for yourself, like a boat. **The point is that whatever your goals may be, the safest way to assure that you don't fall short of them is to invest in inflation-protected bonds.**

Why Plan?

In Chapter 1, you met John and Joan Parker, who thought they were all set for an early retirement, but they were not. **They had a plan—one that failed them.** When the stock market collapsed, they had to cancel their plans for early retirement.

Imagine you, like the Parkers, are well within sight of your retirement goal and find you have to accept five or more years of work. Perhaps your children reach the age when they are ready to go to college, like Bob and Sandy Adams, and that education must be delayed, or the school the child desires to attend must be replaced by one the family can afford.

How can the Parkers and the Adams use the new rules of investing to ensure that they will reach their goals? The answer is by
investing in inflation-protected bonds. In this chapter, you will
learn how these bonds work and how to compute the amount
you will need to invest in them to safely reach your goals.

Inflation Risk

Maybe your parents never preached Benjamin Franklin's motto,
"A penny saved is a penny earned." Or maybe you were never
taken by the hand down to a bank when you were a child to open
your first savings account. Nevertheless, if you're reading this
book, you know the importance of investing at least some of your
savings in assets promising a return that is virtually risk-free in
purchasing power terms. Why is that? Because you realize that it
is quite possible for inflation to outstrip the amount of interest
you gain through a traditional bank savings account, Certificate
of Deposit (CD), or Treasury Bills (T-bills).

No one can accurately predict the rate of inflation. To see why,
take a look at Figure 2.1, which shows the history of inflation in
the United States over 75 years, from 1926 to 2000. The average
annual rate of inflation over this period was 3.17%.

As Figure 2.1 makes clear, the inflation rate is anything but constant. It was as high as 18.2% in 1946, when the price controls
that were imposed during World War Two were removed. There
was a deflation of more than 10% in 1932 during the depths of
the Great Depression.

CONSUMER PRICE INDEX

The measure of inflation most often used—and the one used here—is the Department of Labor's Consumer Price Index, known as the CPI. The CPI is a measure of the average change over time in prices paid by consumers for a fixed market basket of consumer goods and services. The Bureau of Labor Statistics bases the CPI on the prices of about 90,000 items. The broadest, most comprehensive CPI is the Consumer Price Index for All Urban Consumers (CPI-U).

In Figures 2.2 and 2.3, you can see the impact of inflation over periods of 10 years. Figure 2.2 shows that over many 10-year periods inflation increased the cost of living significantly. In the

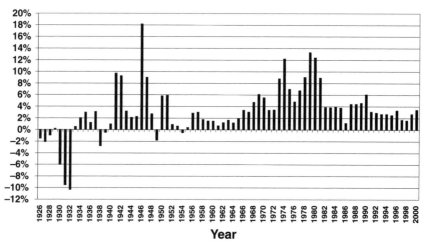

Figure 2.1
Inflation: 1926–2000.

Inflation

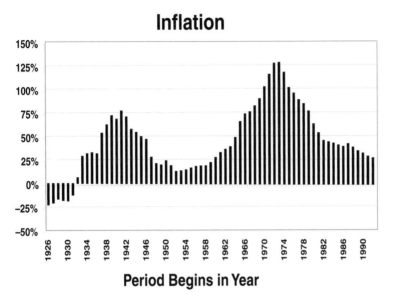

Period Begins in Year

Figure 2.2
Inflation can increase the cost of living
significantly.

worst 10-year period, from January 1973 to December 1982, the
cost of a basket of commonly purchased goods and services
increased by 130%. The average annual inflation rate over that
period was 8.7% per year. Figure 2.3 shows that during that
period, a dollar dropped in purchasing power to about 42 cents.

That's a huge cut in purchasing power over a 10-year period if
you are on a fixed income. On the other hand, for the 10-year
period from January 1926 to December 1935, consumer prices
fell at the average annual rate of 2.5% per year. The purchasing

Purchasing Power of a Dollar

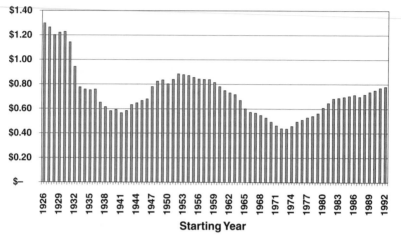

Figure 2.3
Purchasing power of a dollar.

power of the dollar actually increased by almost 30% during this period.

The most important information revealed in Figures 2.1, 2.2, and 2.3 is that prices are rarely stable. Inflation is generally lurking in the economy, mostly weakly, but sometimes strongly. To protect yourself against inflation, it might seem you should forecast what you expect inflation to be over your investment horizon, adjust the target amount you need to save for that expected inflation, and save toward that higher target. As you can see from the chart, inflation varies greatly from year to year and from decade to decade, however, so forecasting it is a very difficult task. Even the Federal Reserve Board, whose responsibility it is to control inflation, finds it nearly impossible.

Now here is the good news: Since you plan to invest in I Bonds, you do not have to make a forecast of the rate of inflation! The reason is that I Bonds pay a fixed rate of interest plus whatever the rate of inflation turns out to be from their date of purchase for up to 30 years. **This means that your investment in I Bonds is not only fully protected against inflation, it is guaranteed to beat inflation by the promised fixed rate.**

The Ins and Outs of I Bonds

Take a closer look at how I Bonds work. Here is a list of their key features:

· They are U.S. Treasury securities backed by the full faith and credit of the U.S. government.

· They are sold at face value and grow with inflation-indexed earnings for up to 30 years.

· They are liquid and can be turned into cash any time after six months.

· You can invest as little as $50 or as much as $30,000 per year.

· **They have a significant tax advantage.**

Let's explore the tax advantage of I Bonds a little further. You can defer Federal taxes on interest earnings for up to 30 years, and I Bonds are completely exempt from state and local income taxes. You don't need to hold them in a special retirement or college savings account to get these benefits. **You can enjoy these tax advantages regardless of how much tax-sheltered saving you do in other special accounts.**

The fixed rate is a rate selected by the U.S. Treasury. It is announced twice a year, at the beginning of May and November. The fixed rate that is in effect when a bond is issued applies until the bond stops increasing in value upon reaching the end of its maturity period, 30 years after its issue date. Thus, the most recently announced fixed rate applies only to bonds purchased during the six months following its announcement. Table 2.1 shows the fixed rates that have been set in the past. The rate by May of 2002 was 2% per year. You can find the current rates at the Treasury's Web site (*www.ustreas.gov*).

Table 2.1   Fixed Rate of Past I Bonds

Date	Fixed Rates*
May 1, 2002	2.00%
Nov.1, 2001	2.00%
May 1, 2001	3.00%
Nov. 1, 2000	3.40%

Table 2.1 Fixed Rate of Past I Bonds (Continued)

Date	Fixed Rates*
May 1, 2000	3.60%
Nov. 1, 1999	3.40%
May 1, 1999	3.30%
Nov. 1, 1998	3.30%

annual rates compounded semiannually

The U.S. Treasury credits I Bonds monthly with a composite rate
of interest that reflects the combined effects of the fixed rate
(which depends on when the bonds were issued) and the semiannual inflation rate (which is the same for all bonds regardless of
when they were issued). The semiannual inflation rate reflects the
percentage change in the CPI-U over a six-month period. It is
announced twice a year, in May and November. The semiannual
inflation rate announced in May reflects the percentage change
between the CPI-U figures from the preceding September and
March. Similarly, the semiannual inflation rate announced in
November reflects the percentage change between the CPI-U
figures from the preceding March and September. As you can see,
there is a delay between the months covered in a measurement
period and the date of the inflation rate announcement.

Deflation will cause a bond to increase in value slowly or not
increase in value at all. **However, even if deflation**

becomes so great that it would reduce the composite rate to below zero, the U.S. Treasury won't allow the value of a bond to decrease from its most recent redemption value. If you redeem a bond that is less than five years old, you'll forfeit the three most recent months' interest on that bond. However, the bond's redemption value will never be less than what you paid for it.[1]

WHO CAN OWN I BONDS?

You can own I Bonds if you have a valid U.S. Social Security number, and you're a resident of the United States, a citizen of the United States, a civilian employee of the United States, regardless of residence, or a worker in the United States. (**Note:** If your career plans include becoming Secretary of the Treasury or the Treasurer of the United States, you should know that while you're in one of those jobs, you can't buy I Bonds!)

TIPS

The other inflation-protected security issued by the U.S. Treasury is TIPS. Officially called Treasury Inflation-Indexed Securities

---

1. The regulations and additional informal guidance on savings bonds are available from the Internet site of the Treasury Department's Bureau of the Public Debt, *www.savingsbonds.gov.* The site also includes a savings bond calculator and a download-able program called the Savings Bond Wizard that allow you to keep track of the current redemption value of all savings bonds you may have purchased since 1941.

(TIIS), these bonds are generally referred to as TIPS. The following is a summary of the key features of these securities:

· The interest rate, which is set at auction, remains fixed
throughout the term of the security.

· The principal amount of the security is adjusted for inflation,
but the inflation-adjusted principal will not be paid until
maturity.

· Semiannual interest payments are based on the inflation-
adjusted principal at the time the interest is paid.

· At maturity, the securities will be redeemed at the greater of
their inflation-adjusted principal or par amount at original
issue.

· Generally, the interest payments are taxable when received.
The inflation adjustments to the principal are taxable in the
year in which such adjustments occur even though the
inflation adjustments will not be paid until maturity.

TIPS work like other marketable Treasury notes and bonds,
except that the fixed rate of interest the U.S. Treasury pays is
applied to your principal after it has been adjusted for inflation
(in accordance with the CPI). So, if inflation occurs throughout
the life of the security, interest payments to you will be greater
each time they are paid.

For example, a 10-year TIPS issue scheduled to mature in January
2012 bears a yield of 2.75%, while a conventional 10-year

Treasury issue slated to mature in February 2012 has a yield of 4.46%. If inflation over the next 10 years averages 1.71% or higher, you make a better gain with a TIPS issue than with traditional T-bills.

If you hold TIPS until they mature, your investments are virtually risk-free. Their purchasing power will keep pace with the broad basket of goods you will buy for everyday living, and the U.S. government will always make its interest payments and principal repayments when the bonds mature. In addition, they pay a return above inflation.

Unlike I Bonds, which you can redeem whenever you want according to a schedule of rising constant-dollar prices that are known in advance, TIPS have a fixed maturity date and can be redeemed only at that date. If you want the cash, you can sell TIPS to another investor. The price, however, is not known in advance, and therefore TIPS are safe only if you hold them to maturity.

There is also an important difference between the way the interest earned on I Bonds and TIPS is treated for income tax purposes by the Internal Revenue Service (IRS). The interest on I Bonds is not taxed until you cash them in, which may be as long as 30 years in the future. But interest earned on TIPS, even if it is only accrued interest, is taxable on a yearly basis unless they are held in an Individual Retirement Account (IRA), 401(k), or other retirement account.

Because the tax treatment of I Bonds is more favorable, the interest rate on I Bonds is set lower than the rate on TIPS. However, you can avoid paying taxes on TIPS by holding them in a retirement account, such as an IRA or 401(k) plan. For this purpose, TIPS are preferable to I Bonds. Many mutual fund companies that provide investment products for IRAs and 401(k) plans now offer TIPS funds as one of the choices.

How to Compute the Amount You Need to Invest

Let's say you are saving money to buy a sailboat that now costs $50,000. You want to buy it 10 years from now. To compute how much you need to invest, you need two critical pieces of information:

- How much will the boat cost at the target date, 10 years from now?
- What rate of interest can you earn on the money you invest?

You are not sure what the boat will actually cost at the target date. All you know is that you are pretty sure its price will go up in tandem with the general rate of inflation.

From Figures 2.2 and 2.3, you conclude that over the next 10 years, inflation could turn out to be as high as 8.7% per year, which is what it was during the period from 1973 to 1982. At that rate of inflation, the boat would cost $115,150 10 years from now.

Let's say you decide to earmark a certain amount of money now for the purchase of your sailboat. You dub it the "sailboat fund," and you plan to invest it all in I Bonds. How much must you invest in order to have the $50,000 that you will need 10 years from now?

We will assume that the fixed real rate of interest on I Bonds is 2% per year. You can do all your calculations using this 2% interest rate and ignore inflation. The result you get will be correct no matter what the actual inflation rate turns out to be.

COMPUTING THE AMOUNT YOU NEED

There are several ways to compute the amount needed. Here are three alternative methods:

Method 1: Multiplication and division. Each year your fund will be worth 1.02 times what it was worth the year before. Let X be the amount you need to invest. Then at the end of one year, you will have 1.02 times X. At the end of two years, you will have 1.02 x 1.02 x X, which is 1.02^2 times X. And at the end of 10 years, you will have 1.02^{10} times X, which is 1.21899442 X. Finally, to find X divide $50,000 by 1.21899442, and you get $41,017.41.

Method 2: Use the following mathematical formula derived from the process described in Method 1:

$$PV = \frac{FV}{(1+i)^n}$$

COMPUTING THE AMOUNT YOU NEED (CONTINUED)

PV stands for present value, *FV* for future value, *i* for the interest rate, and *n* for the number of years. In our case, *FV* is $50,000, *i* is .02, and *n* is 10. Substituting them into the formula, you find that the present value is $41,017.41.

$$PV = \frac{\$50,000}{(1.02)^{10}} = \$41,017.41$$

Method 3: Use the interactive Worry-Free Investing (WFI) calculator provided on this book's companion Web site (*www.prenhall.com/worryfree/*). It looks like this:

WFI Present Value Calculator

Number of years	10
Interest rate	2%
Future value	$50,000
Present value	**$41,017.41**

You type in the number of years, the interest rate, and the future value, and then the WFI calculator computes the present value for you.

No matter which method you use to compute the amount, if you invest $41,017.41 in I Bonds now and redeem them in 10 years, you will receive an amount of cash worth $50,000 in today's dollars.[2] The actual amount of cash you receive when you redeem the I Bonds will depend on the rate of inflation over the 10 years. For example, if the rate of inflation turns out to be 8% per year, then you will receive $107,946 when you cash in your I Bonds. But remember the assumption that the price of the boat goes up by the same amount as the CPI, so when you go to buy the boat, it should cost you $107,946.

REVIEW QUESTION

To test your understanding, you can try it out assuming that the rate of interest on I Bonds is 3% per year instead of 2%. How much would you need to invest to have enough to buy the boat 10 years from now?

Let X be the amount you need to invest. Then at the end of 10 years, you will have 1.03^{10} times X, which is 1.3439164X. To find X, divide $50,000 by 1.3439164, and you get $37,204.70.

What if instead of investing a lump sum now, you plan to fund your purchase of the boat by buying equal amounts of I Bonds over each of the next 10 years? There is an element of risk, namely the risk that the real rate of interest on I Bonds (i.e., the promised fixed rate that is added to inflation) could go down. As you have

---

2. Since the minimum denomination I Bond is $50, you would round off your investment to $41,000.

seen, this rate has changed quite a bit in the past. It has been as high as 3.6% and was at the time of this writing lower. You have no way of knowing whether it will go up, down, or stay the same in the future.

Despite this risk of changes in the I Bond real interest rate, investing in I Bonds is still the safest strategy you can pursue. In the shaded area below, we show how to compute the annual contribution required in dollars of today's purchasing power to achieve the desired target. The annual contribution is $4,476.80.

COMPUTING THE ANNUAL AMOUNT YOU NEED TO CONTRIBUTE

To compute the annual amount you will need to contribute to your fund, let's assume that the I Bond real interest rate will remain at 2% per year. Again, there are three ways to calculate your annual contribution:

Method 1: Multiplication and division. Let X be your annual contribution to the fund. Assuming that you start your contributions immediately, the first year's contribution will grow by the end of 10 years to $1.02^{10} X$, the second year's contribution will grow to $1.02^9 X$, and so on until the last year's contribution, which will grow to $1.02 X$. Thus at the end of 10 years you will have a total of:

$$(1.02+1.02^2+1.02^3+1.02^4+1.02^5+1.02^6+1.02^7+1.02^8+1.02^9+$$
$$1.02^{10}) X = 11.16871542 X$$

COMPUTING THE ANNUAL AMOUNT YOU NEED
TO CONTRIBUTE (CONTINUED)

Since you want to have $50,000 at the end of 10 years, you find X by dividing $50,000 by 11.16871542:

$$\$50,000 \ / \ 11.16871542 = \$4,476.80$$

Method 2: Use the following mathematical formula derived from the process described in Method 1:

$$FV = \frac{(1+i)^{n+1} - (1+i)}{i} X$$

FV stands for future value, i for the interest rate, n for the number of years, and X for the annual contribution. In this case, FV is $50,000, i is.02, and n is 10. Substituting these figures into the formula, you find that the annual contribution X is $4,476.80:

$$FV = \frac{(1.02)^{11} - (1.02)}{.02} X = \$50,000$$

$$11.16871542X = \$50,000$$

$$X = \frac{\$50,000}{11.16871542} = \$4,476.80$$

Method 3: Use the interactive WFI calculator provided on this book's companion Web site. It looks like this:

COMPUTING THE ANNUAL AMOUNT YOU NEED TO CONTRIBUTE (CONTINUED)

WFI Saving Calculator

Number of years	10
Interest rate	2%
Future value	$50,000
Present value	**$4,476.80**

You type in the number of years, the interest rate, and the future value, then the WFI calculator computes the annual contribution for you.

You have looked at how no investing strategy is completely free of risk, but that with I Bonds and TIPS it is possible to get close. To figure out how much to invest in inflation-protected securities in order to reach your target, you need to know your real rate of interest (net of inflation). You do not have to forecast the average rate of inflation.

Now that you have the basic concept of how to take account of inflation and how to reach your investment goals safely, you explore ways of investing safely for retirement in the next chapter.

3

Reaching Your Retirement Goal

In this chapter, you explore:

· How to invest for retirement

· How to ensure that your income lasts for as long as you live

· How to minimize income taxes and fees paid to brokers and money managers

Harriet Beach always came home to her two-bedroom Rhode Island home with fewer groceries than she wanted. She bought day-old bread and clipped coupons. She put off travel, even to see the last remaining members of her family, and kept the phone calls to them short. She and her husband had saved for years, using savings, mutual funds, his 401(k), and a number of other means. She had thousands set aside to draw from.

Still, each night, Harriet went to bed and visualized a whirl of worries swirling across the ceiling—so chilling to her that even Stephen King couldn't top the horror. She lived in constant fear! There was inflation, Social Security, and as sure as death, taxes. What if something happened? Would she have enough? The worst of it was, she lived in a fear she did not have to experience.

In this chapter, you will learn how to invest your retirement savings so that, unlike Harriet, you can sleep peacefully at night. We explain how to take account of each important factor: inflation, life expectancy, Social Security, income taxes, and management fees.

The Retirement Goal

Ensuring that you will be able to afford a comfortable retirement involves three steps.

1. Setting a goal—establishing a target amount of income you will need each year in retirement
2. Saving enough to achieve that goal
3. Investing your savings in a way that guarantees that you will reach your goal

Consider the following example. Let's assume you are currently 35 years old, expect to retire in 30 years at age 65, and live for 20 more years until the age of 85. Your current labor income is $50,000 per year, and you have not yet accumulated any assets.

Experts recommend that to maintain your standard of living in retirement, you should aim for a replacement rate equal to 70% of your preretirement salary before taxes. Why not 100%? The main reason is that once you retire, you will not be saving for retirement any more.

Let's accept 70% as your target replacement rate. But, remember, **you want to be sure that your retirement income will keep pace with inflation and last for as long as you live.** That means you will have to accumulate enough during your working years to provide a retirement income that rises with inflation. **Social Security benefits are automatically adjusted each year for increases in the cost of living, but private pension benefits usually are not.** Many people overlook this important fact and wind up with less retirement income than they need in their later years.

For now, we'll simplify the example by ignoring taxes. Also, let's assume that your *real* income from your job, that is, your job-related income adjusted for inflation, remains at $50,000 per year until age 65. In other words, we assume that your income will keep pace with inflation, but not beat it. With a real income before retirement of $50,000, the target level of retirement income is .7 x $50,000 or $35,000 per year.

How much should you save?

Every dollar you save will earn interest until you take it out. Of course, the cost of living will be going up, too. We assume that you will invest in Treasury Inflation-Protected Securities (TIPS), earning a fixed rate of 3% per year plus whatever the rate of inflation turns out to be. In other words, the *real* rate of interest is 3% per year.

The method for computing the saving rate needed to reach the desired target consists of two steps:

1. **Compute the amount you need to have accumulated in your personal retirement account when you reach retirement age.**

2. **Compute the annual saving needed to reach that future value.**

So, first compute the amount that you must have in your retirement fund at age 65 to be able to withdraw $35,000 per year for 20 years. Remember, the money you have in the account will continue to earn 3% a year, after inflation, as long as it's in the account.

COMPUTING THE AMOUNT YOU NEED

To calculate the amount needed, we can either use a formula or the Worry-Free Investing (WFI) calculator at our companion Web site. The formula is:[*]

$$PV = \frac{1 - \dfrac{1}{(1+i)^n}}{i} X$$

PV stands for the present value of the stream of benefits, i for the interest rate, n for the number of years, and X for the annual benefit. In our case i is .03, n is 20, and X is \$35,000. Substituting them into the formula, you find that the present value is:

$$PV = \frac{1 - \dfrac{1}{1.03^{20}}}{.03} \times \$35,000$$
$$= 14.87747486 \times \$35,000$$
$$= \$520,712$$

Let's use the online WFI calculator to do this:

WFI Calculations for Amount Needed at Retirement

Number of years	20
Interest rate	3%
Target retirement income	\$35,000
Amount required at retirement	**\$520,712**

COMPUTING THE AMOUNT YOU NEED

Thus, you need $520,712 in your account the day you retire to generate $35,000 a year for 20 years, assuming your investments earn 3% return after inflation.

The next step is to calculate how much of your preretirement salary to save each year to reach that goal. You have 30 years until you retire, and you plan to contribute part of your annual salary to your retirement fund each year. By the time you retire, you need to have $520,712. Again, we are assuming you will earn a real interest rate of 3% per year.

We can use the formula we learned in Chapter 2 to find the annual contribution needed to reach a desired future value:[†]

$$FV = \frac{(1+i)^{n+1} - (1+i)}{i} X$$

FV stands for future value, i for the interest rate, n for the number of years, and X for the annual contribution. In this case, FV is $520,712, i is .03, and n is 30. Substituting these figures into the formula, you find that the annual contribution X is $10,626:

$$FV = \frac{(1.03)^{31} - (1.03)}{.03} X = \$520,712$$
$$49.00267818 X = \$520,712$$
$$X = \$10,626$$

Using the online WFI calculator at our Web site (*www.prenhall.com/worryfree/*) to do this, you find:

COMPUTING THE AMOUNT YOU NEED

WFI Calculations for Annual Contributions Required

Number of years	30
Interest rate	3%
Target future value	$520,712
Annual contribution required	**$10,626**

Thus, in order to be able to take out a retirement benefit of $35,000 per year for 20 years, you would need to save $10,626 per year in each of the next 30 years.

*. This is the formula for the present value of an *ordinary annuity*. This means payments start at the *end* of the year.
†. This is the formula for the future value of an *immediate annuity*. This means contributions start immediately, at the *beginning* of the year.

To take account of inflation, you compute the saving rate as a proportion of salary. This is because salaries generally increase at about the rate of inflation, or slightly faster. However, if you are in a declining industry, this might not be so. Assuming you are in a healthy industry, and ignoring the possibility of raises due to promotions, you divide $10,626 by your salary of $50,000, which is 21.25%. Thus, if you save 21.25% of your salary each year, you would be able to pay yourself a retirement income equal to 70% of your preretirement income, or $35,000. Like Social Security benefits, this income will increase in dollar amount each year to maintain its purchasing power no matter what the rate of inflation turns out to be.

Prices of specific goods and services may rise higher than the rate of inflation, but in general they, too, keep pace with the rate of inflation enough for the purposes of your financial planning and goal setting. While inflation varies somewhat depending on where you live and what stage of life you are in, this approach will bring you very close to protecting your retirement purchasing power. If you should move before or during retirement to a low-cost area, you may even come out a little ahead.

In this example, we assumed your salary was $50,000, but suppose it is $100,000. Again, we assume your salary keeps pace with inflation, no more, no less. To achieve a 70% replacement rate by retirement age, you will have to save 21.25% of your salary just like the person who earns $50,000, provided all the other assumptions hold true (i.e., you have 30 years to go before retirement age, a life expectancy of 20 years after retirement, and the real interest rate is 3% per year). In fact, no matter what your salary is, the required saving rate will be the same 21.25% because the required saving rate depends only on the number of years you have to save before retirement, the number of years you will live after retirement, and the real interest rate.

Table 3.1 shows the fraction of your salary you must save for different numbers of years before and after retirement if the real interest rate is 3%.

Table 3.1   Required Saving Rates*

	Years After Retirement			
Years Before Retirement	**10**	**15**	**20**	**25**
15	32%	45%	56%	66%
20	22%	31%	39%	45%
25	16%	23%	29%	33%
30	13%	18%	22%	26%
35	10%	14%	17%	20%
40	8%	11%	14%	16%

Assumptions: The real interest rate is 3% per year and salary keeps pace with inflation before retirement.

Thus, you see from Table 3.1 that with a life expectancy of 20 years after retirement, you would have to save 29% of your salary if you started saving 25 years before retirement instead of 30 years before retirement. That sounds impossible. Who can save 29% of income every year after all of the expenses of daily living? Even those noted savers, the Japanese, don't save that much.

Relax. Whether you know it or not, you already are saving some of that amount in your Social Security account. While you can't get at that money, as you can with most of your other savings, and the government can change the rules at any time, at present you can assume a significant amount of help.[1]

Social Security

How should you take Social Security into account in your retirement planning? The first thing you should recognize is that you have no choice about participating in it. It is a mandatory saving, investment, and insurance system for all residents of the United States. For people who earn lower salaries throughout their lives, it is actually a pretty good deal. For these workers, retirement and survivors' and disability insurance benefits are generous relative to taxes paid over a working career. Furthermore, benefits are largely protected against inflation.

Since Social Security is mandatory, the relevant question is: How much additional voluntary saving and investing must you do in order to provide yourself with your required 70% replacement rate of salary? Each year, the Social Security Administration mails you a statement showing your projected retirement benefit based on your age, current salary, and earnings history. Alternatively, the Social Security Administration provides estimates of your expected retirement benefits at *www.ssa.gov*.

The interactive Quick Calculator found at that site asks you for your current age and earnings. Using the same assumptions as

---

1. Some military, federal, state, and railroad employees as well as teachers in some states' high schools and colleges do not participate, but often have their own retirement systems.

BASIC SOCIAL SECURITY BENEFITS

What determines the basic value of your Social Security benefits?

The answer is your work record. You pay employment tax when you work. Your future benefits depend on a formula that takes into account your earnings and the number of years you have worked and contributed to Social Security. The later you retire, the greater your monthly benefit. The benefit is 33.5% higher if you delay your retirement by four years. A delay of eight years, to age 70, is good for a retirement increase of about 70%. *

*. Ages and information are subject to change and should be confirmed at the Social Security Web site (*www.ssa.gov*).

our earlier example, you would input your current age as 35 and your current earnings as $50,000, as shown in Table 3.2

Table 3.2 Social Security Benefit Quick Calculator

Quick Calculator

Benefit estimates depend on your age and on your earnings history. Below you need to enter:

1. The age you will attain by the end of this year (must be between **ages 22 and 62**), and

2. Your current annual earnings (must be earnings **covered by Social Security**)

Table 3.2   Social Security Benefit Quick Calculator

Quick Calculator

Enter age attained by the end of this year: <u>35</u>
Enter earnings in the current year: <u>$50,000</u>
Select to see your benefit estimate in today's dollars, or inflated (future) dollars

Quick Calculator: Estimated Benefits

Estimates are based on the information you submitted:
Age in 2002: **35 (born 1967)**
Current earnings: **$50,000**
Benefit in **year-2002** dollars:

Retirement age	Monthly benefit amount
62 in 2029	$1,104
67 in 2034	$1,592
70 in 2037	$1,980

Using the Quick Calculator at the Social Security site, you discover that your level of benefits depends on the age at which you retire. You can start drawing benefits as early as age 62 with a monthly benefit of $1,104 ($13,248 per year). If you wait until age 67 the benefit will be $1,592 per month ($19,104 per year), and at a starting age of 70 it will be $1,980 per month ($23,760 per year).

This means that to achieve your desired level of $35,000 per year in retirement income, you need to save much less than the 21.25% of salary we computed earlier. How much less?

Note that between ages 62 and 67, the starting benefit level rises about $1,171 per year. Between ages 67 and 70, it rises by $1,552 per year. We will assume that if you retire at 65, your Social Security benefit will be $16,761. That is 48% of the $35,000 in target retirement income that you wanted. Your retirement fund will have to provide the other 52%.

That means you will need to save 52% of the required amount we computed earlier. In other words, instead of saving 21.25% of your salary, you only need to save .52 times 21.25%, which is 11% of your salary. That may be hard, but not impossible.

Employer-Sponsored Pensions

If you work for an employer that has a pension plan, you should take account of pension benefits in the same way we just showed to take account of Social Security benefits. For example, let's say that by the time you retire you will have worked for your employer for 30 years. A typical defined benefit pension plan provides a pension based on salary and years of service, and a typical formula would be 1.4% of your final pay per year of service (though some are higher and some are lower). In this case, that would be 1.4 x 30 = 42% of your $50,000 salary. That is, your pension plan will pay you $21,000 per year.

However, you must adjust the pension amount due to the fact that while Social Security benefits are indexed to the cost of living, most employer pension benefits are not. Inflation will erode the value of that $21,000 a year after you retire. So you will still need to save to offset the possible effect of inflation on your pension benefits.

If you are able to take your pension as a lump sum, rather than as a monthly payment, you could use the large sum of money you will receive to invest in something that protects against inflation in the same way that Social Security does.

Employers often provide incentives to save for retirement by matching part of voluntary employee contributions in such vehicles as 401(k), 403(b), and 457 plans. Failing to take advantage of these voluntary savings plans means you will need to save much more on your own. In addition, the government offers large tax breaks if you save through special retirement savings accounts such as 401(k) plans.

You can add further to your retirement savings by using Individual Retirement Accounts (IRAs). You may be able to deduct your contributions to your IRA from your taxes, but even if you can't, the investment earnings aren't taxed until you retire, so your IRA assets grow more quickly than if they were taxed as they occurred.

Guaranteeing That Your Income Lasts as Long as You Do

After you retire and start living off your investments, a major risk is that your money will run out before you do. Social Security benefits last for as long as you live, so not only do they protect you against inflation, they also protect against the risk of outliving your resources. You can turn your retirement fund into homemade Social Security at retirement by buying a Single-Premium Immediate Annuity (SPIA).

SPIAs are sold by insurance companies. The insurance company charges a price that reflects your life expectancy, and its shareholders absorb the risk that you and its other customers may live longer than expected.[2] By pooling the mortality risk of many customers, the insurance company's shareholders face much less risk than the customers.

Some people dislike the fact that when you buy a life annuity contract, no money is left after you die. You can buy a joint-life annuity that provides a lifetime income for two people, presumably you and your spouse. However, SPIAs are not designed to provide a bequest to children or your other relatives; they are designed to maximize the income payable to the annuitants.

Most SPIAs are not indexed to inflation, so their monthly payments do not automatically increase as the cost of living rises. A few American companies[3] did offer inflation-proof annuities, but withdrew them as of March 2003, though they may offer them again in the future in the United States. Check regularly for these if obtaining annuities indexed for inflation is part of your desired worry-free approach, which you can consider by examining Table 3.3.

---

2. To get an online quote for an SPIA, you can visit *www.brkdirect.com/spia/EZQuote.asp*.
3. Companies that do offer inflation-proof annuities can be found via the Internet in other countries, such as Switzerland, India, and the U.K. (e.g., Prudential UK), but these have not been traditionally available to anyone outside those countries.

Table 3.3 shows the guaranteed lifetime inflation-proof income you could purchase for $100,000 at different starting ages.

Table 3.3   Inflation-Proof Lifetime Income per $100,000 of Retirement Wealth*

Starting Age	Inflation-Proof Annual Income	Life Expectancy for a Single Life (IRS Pub 590)
45	$3,924	83.8 yrs
55	$4,692	84.6 yrs
65	$6,036	86.0 yrs
75	$8,568	87.5 yrs

These rates applied in August 2002. They will change as interest rates and life expectancies change.

The last column of Table 3.3 shows the life expectancy for a single person. Your personal life expectancy may be different because of your gender, family history, health, diet, and other habits. Some Web sites offer free online calculators to compute your life expectancy based on these factors. One insurance company has even made a game out of it.[4]

---

4. See the Longevity Game at *www.northwesternmutual.com/corporate/newsmedia/ longevitygame.html.*

IS AN SPIA RIGHT FOR YOU?

Who should buy an SPIA? You can do a break-even calculation to judge whether you think it is right for you. Here is how.

Compute your life expectancy at retirement. Let's say you expect to retire at age 65 and your life expectancy is 86. Then your expected number of years in retirement is 21.

Look up the SPIA income you can receive for a one-time investment of $100,000. From Table 3.3, we see that you can receive $6,036 per year in inflation-proof income guaranteed to last for life.

Now compute the amount you could withdraw each year from a $100,000 retirement fund invested in TIPS earning a real interest rate of 3% per year assuming 21 annual withdrawals. The formula is:

$$X = \frac{i}{1 - \dfrac{1}{(1+i)^n}} \times \$100,000$$

IS AN SPIA RIGHT FOR YOU? (CONTINUED)

X is the annual amount you can withdraw, i is the real interest rate, and n is the number of withdrawals. Substituting into the formula, we find that the annual withdrawal is $6,487.

$$X = \frac{.03}{1 - \dfrac{1}{(1.03)^{21}}} \times \$100,000$$

$$= .06487 \times \$100,000$$

$$= \$6,487$$

Comparing the two numbers, $6,487 versus $6,036, we see that you would have to give up $451 per year if you bought the SPIA. But, remember, in return for the $451 difference you have the guarantee that should you live to 100, you would still be receiving an inflation-proof income from the insurance company.

Income Taxes

As Benjamin Franklin said: "In this world nothing is certain but death and taxes."

However, as inevitable as taxes are, **there are ways for you to reduce them. The U.S. government tries to encourage retirement saving by offering breaks that can save you a lot in taxes. The contributions you make to a qualified retirement plan are deducted from your taxable income, and the interest you earn on the**

money in the retirement account is not taxed. You only pay income taxes when you withdraw money from the account after you retire.

If you are not covered by an employer-sponsored tax-deferred plan, such as a 401(k), or you are covered but your income is less than $54,000 a year ($34,000 a year if you are single), you can set up a tax-deferred IRA. By setting up a tax-deferred IRA, you can contribute up to $3,000 a year ($3,500 a year if you are aged 50 or more), deduct your contributions from your taxable income, and invest the money in inflation-protected bonds to earn a real interest rate of 3% per year. Your spouse can also contribute up to $3,000 a year if he or she is not covered by a retirement plan.

When you take the money out after retirement, you will have to pay taxes. If you are covered by a retirement plan, you can still start an IRA, but your contributions must be made with after-tax dollars. However, the investment earnings on the assets in your IRA are still tax-deferred.[5]

The result is that every dollar you save and invest in your IRA allows you to transfer taxable income from your working years (ages 35–64) to your retirement years (ages 65–85).

There are three advantages to the IRA for those who can deduct their contributions:

---

5. In the case of Roth IRAs, where you are using after-tax dollars to invest, any qualified distribution, including investment earnings, is not taxable instead of being tax-deferred.

1. **You lower your taxes while you are working and saving for retirement.**

2. **You will probably be in a lower tax bracket after you retire.**

3. **You earn a higher real return on your retirement savings. The government, in effect, is subsidizing your saving.**

The first two of these advantages require no explanation, but the third one does. If you were to buy the U.S. Treasury's Inflation-Indexed Securities (TIPS) outside the framework of an IRA or another retirement plan, you would have to pay income taxes on the interest earned as you earn it. Thus, if you had to pay income tax at the rate of 20% on the interest you earn, instead of earning 3% per year you would earn only 2.4% per year (.8 x 3% = 2.4%). But as long as the money is in a retirement account, you pay no taxes on it.

This makes a very big difference to the amount of saving you need to do for retirement. This applies to anyone who saves through an IRA, whether you can deduct the contribution or not.

Transaction Costs

Transaction costs, such as brokerage fees and commissions, are a very real part of your considerations when you plan for retirement. Almost all investments have fees and transaction costs associated with them.

Mutual funds, for example, have transaction costs that fall into two categories: loads and management expenses. A *load* is a sales charge that is paid once, whereas *management expenses* are recurring annual costs. Front-end loads are levied when you deposit money into a mutual fund, and back-end loads, also called *redemption fees*, are exacted when you withdraw money. A typical load is around 3%. If you invest $1,000 in a mutual fund with a 3% load, only $970 actually gets invested to work for you. The remaining $30 goes to the mutual fund company to pay its sales force and the advisor who sold you the fund.

You can avoid loads by investing in no-load funds, but you will still have the annual expenses that pay the fund managers' salaries. The median expense ratio is about 1% of assets, and it is paid every year.

Mutual funds that invest in TIPS have expenses that are much lower than for funds that invest in conventional stocks and bonds. Vanguard's Inflation-Protected Securities fund, for example, has an expense ratio of only .25%. It is therefore not surprising that the fund companies do little to advertise their TIPS funds.

Economy of Motion Savings

Let's return for a moment to the case of Harriet Beach of Rhode Island, who was mentioned earlier. Her mother lived through the Depression, and all Harriet heard about for years were stories of people canning their foods, and lucky to have that. She and her husband saved and saved, using every means in their power: a money market account, CDs, mutual funds, some money in a stocks portfolio, and a 401(k) at her husband's job for a publishing company. By the time her husband had died, the week before his retirement party, they had a reasonable amount of money set aside to live comfortably. With no children, Harriet might have realized her lifelong wish to travel to Europe, and perhaps Asia.

Unfortunately, Harriet had a fear bigger than her dreams. She was afraid all the money she and her husband had saved would not be enough. Every year, the purchasing power of the dollar decreased. She could remember when a new car cost less than a bad day at the dentist these days. What if she had to go in for assisted living? What if she suffered a major catastrophic illness? The sad ending is that two weeks after her 72nd birthday, Harriet died in her sleep. A large part of what was left of her estate, $247,000 in savings, went to the IRS and the state government.

Let's face it, Harriet was a bit of a worrywort. But her fears reflect those of many who face retirement. So here's the important thing about saving with TIPS, I Bonds, and inflation-proof annuities. **You do not have to worry about inflation at all. In fact, you might find you even need to save less.** If Harriet had the opportunity to buy an inflation-proof annuity, maybe she would have kicked up her heels a bit and flown to the Greek Isles as she'd always dreamed of doing.

In this chapter, you have explored how you can focus low-risk investment principles toward your retirement. TIPS, I Bonds, and inflation-proof annuities provide real returns immune to two of the chief causes of retirement fund erosion: inflation and transaction costs.

Social Security is a mandatory retirement plan that provides benefits in return for the taxes you pay during your working career. Don't forget to take account of those benefits in planning how much to save.

Employers often provide incentives to save for retirement by matching part of voluntary employee contributions in such vehicles as 401(k), 403(b), and 457 plans. Failing to take advantage of these voluntary savings plans means you will need to save much more on your own. In addition, the government offers large tax breaks if you save through special retirement savings accounts such as 401(k) plans.

You can add further to your retirement savings by using IRAs. You may be able to deduct your contributions to your IRA from your taxes, but even if you can't, the investment earnings aren't taxed until you retire, so your IRA assets grow more quickly than if they were taxed as they occurred.

You can save a lot of money on broker commissions and money manager fees by investing directly in TIPS,

I Bonds, and inflation-proof annuities. If you target your risk-free investments to achieve your goals, you do not need to save as much. This is because when you take big investment risks you need to save a lot to have a safety cushion.

In Chapter 4, you will look at how to invest with your children's college education as the goal.

C H A P T E R

4

Investing Safely
for College

In this chapter you explore:

· How tuition costs often increase at a greater rate than inflation

· Tax-advantaged college investment programs

· Special risks of investing for college—and how to overcome
them

R uthie Sullivan was in her senior year of high school, and
nothing that could happen this school year could be
greater than the letter of acceptance she received from
Stanford University. Her parents, Bill, one of the hardest-working
construction subcontractors in all Pittsburgh, and her librarian
mother, Mary, had saved for years to put Ruthie through college.
The money was in a mix of stock and bond mutual funds offered
by an investment company and earmarked for college savings.

When Ruthie came home one afternoon to find both parents at the kitchen table with piles and forms covering the surface, their glum looks kept her from asking, "What's up?" She sat down cautiously on one of the chairs and said instead, "How bad is it?"

"Have you given thought to Pitt, Penn State, or any other of a number of good schools?" her dad asked.

"You . . . you don't understand a thing about the American Dream, do you?" Ruthie shouted, knocking over the chair as she stood. She ran to her room, locked the door, and threw herself on the bed. Then she felt even worse, since she had been reading newspapers, too, and knew what had happened to the economy.

"I'm a worthless unthankful brat," she cried. Ruthie was smart enough to realize that the American Dream isn't just going to a better school than her parents and that economic downturns are not their fault. She sat up and went to her computer. She'd better start looking into school loans before her folks took out a second mortgage on the house.

High-Priced Item

Aside from your home or your retirement, a college education for a child is probably one of the largest expenditures of your life. Plus, you will need the money before you need your retirement money. Tuition, room, and board for a four-year college can cost between $40,000 and $120,000—per child.

More troubling is the fact that college inflation has exceeded general inflation by a large margin for the last 20 years. Figure 4.1 shows the year-by-year difference between the rate of increase in college costs and general inflation as measured by the Consumer Price Index (CPI). The source of the data is the Bureau of Labor Statistics. The average difference is 4.33% per year.

Perhaps even more troubling than that is the fact that the discrepancy varies a lot from year to year. College costs and the CPI can diverge unpredictably. This means that even investing in I Bonds is not a completely safe way to ensure that you will have what you need when you need it.

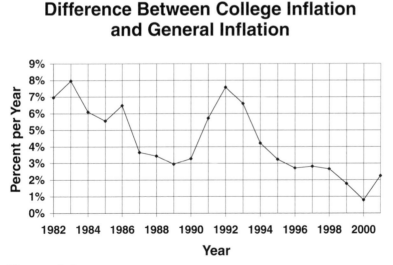

Difference Between College Inflation and General Inflation

Figure 4.1
The difference between college inflation and general inflation.

Fortunately, the federal and state governments have cooperated to offer special tax breaks for funds earmarked for college, and there are investments that are linked to an index of college costs.

Like 401(k), 403b, Individual Retirement Accounts (IRAs), and the other tax-advantaged plans for retirement, the plans earmarked for college have their own peculiar names and numbers. In fact, in the case of the college plans, there are many more names and numbers because every state government has established at least one of them. What matter, however, are the following two features:

1. The tax advantages they offer
2. The investment choices open to you

By far, the two most important types of plans are Section 529 plans and prepaid tuition plans. Below we discuss how they differ with respect to their tax advantages and their investment choices.

Section 529 Plans

When it comes to tax-advantaged college investing, the number to remember is 529. The number comes from the section of the Internal Revenue Code that authorizes it. A Section 529 plan is an investment plan operated by a state and designed to help families save for future college costs. Congress authorized Section 529 investment plans in 1996. Every state now offers at least one 529 plan.

Your 529 investment grows tax-free for as long as your money stays in the plan. And when the plan makes a distribution to pay for the beneficiary's college costs, the distribution is federal tax-free as well.[1] Your own state may also offer some tax breaks (like an upfront deduction for your contributions or income exemption on withdrawals) in addition to the federal treatment. In New York, for example, the tax deduction is $10,000 per parent per year. Be sure to check with your own state about tax incentives and limitations.

In many states, you can even adjust the investment portfolio linked to your 529 plan. If you prefer a more conservative approach, you can speak with the agent with whom you set up the plan and make appropriate adjustments.

Section 529 plans also have financial-aid advantages. Assets in these plans are not considered a student asset in the formulas used to determine financial aid. Withdrawals can be made tax-free, and no 1099 form is sent out.

Although each state sets its own rules for these plans, **the money in a Section 529 investment plan can be used for college expenses at any accredited college in any state.** Moreover, they are usually open to residents of any other state. Also, in many cases, the money from 529 plans can be used on public and private schools outside the issuing state (you need to check with each state's plan).

---

1. This treatment applies for distributions in the years 2002–2010.

By contrast, prepaid tuition plans are strictly for the residents of one state and apply only to in-state schools. If the amount is transferred to the college of another state, the tuition guarantee may not hold. For example, if you enroll in the Texas Guaranteed Tuition Plan,[2] and your child goes to the University of Massachusetts, you may discover that the amount you receive from the Texas fund is not enough to pay tuition in Massachusetts. You should check with each plan to learn its limitations before investing.

Section 529 plan assets can be transferred between family beneficiaries. If one child doesn't use the money for college, you can designate another recipient. It can even be a niece or nephew. Grandparents who set up the plans can switch the money between grandchildren. The giver retains control over the assets until they are distributed to pay for college.

The contributor does not have to be a parent, grandparent, or even a relative. You can make a contribution for any living beneficiary who plans to attend college. **If you're an adult and plan to attend law or medical school, you can contribute your own savings to a Section 529 plan.**

Other college savings plans either limit the amount of contributions each year or place restrictions on parental income. Section 529 plans have very high limits: a one-time $50,000 contribution per donor and state-imposed maximum total contribution limits

---

2. For more details about the Texas plan, see *www.tgtp.org/overview.html*.

that range as high as Rhode Island's $246,000 (although earnings can grow the account beyond that amount).

Investment Choices and Risks

After reading the previous chapters of this book, you are probably wondering about the risk of the investments in 529 plans and other college plans. The answer varies from state to state, and the differences are great. The vast majority of states have contracted with financial service firms to offer a selection of mutual funds. These funds are all risky. There are only two states that have a truly safe investment option in their 529 plans—Arizona and Montana. That option is CollegeSure® CDs.

CollegeSure® CDs

The CollegeSure® CD is a Certificate of Deposit linked to college costs and guaranteed to meet future tuition, fees, room, and board. It is offered by College Savings Bank, and it pays an annual interest rate tied to the rise in college costs each year. Principal and interest are FDIC-insured—backed by the U.S. government—up to $100,000 per depositor. The interest rate of these CDs is pegged to annual increases in college education costs, as measured by an index of such average costs established by gathering data from 500 independent colleges. Over the term to maturity of each CollegeSure® CD, the annual interest rate you will earn is guaranteed to be not less than 3%.

Each CD deposit of $250 or more is measured in terms of units. Units are a measure of how much college you've prepaid so that you can keep track of your progress. One unit, at maturity, is equal to one full year's average tuition, fees, room, and board at a four-year private college as measured by the Independent College 500® Index (IC 500). The purchase price per unit exceeds the value of the IC 500 at the deposit date.

For example, if today's cost for one year of private college is $26,740, you would deposit $30,840 to purchase one unit of a CollegeSure® CD for your three-year-old child to guarantee the future cost of college in fifteen years. At maturity, you'll receive one year of whatever private college costs are in fifteen years, no matter how high college costs rise.

Age-Based College Funds

Investment companies have created so-called age-based portfolios intended for 529 plans and other college accounts. These funds typically offer a portfolio whose asset mix is predetermined to change year by year. The proportion invested in stocks starts out high and declines as the number of years left grows smaller.

A defining feature of these plans is that their asset mix does *not* depend on how the securities in the portfolio perform over time. Whether the stocks or bonds in the portfolio go up or down in value, the fractions invested in each asset class are readjusted each year according to a predetermined schedule.

If the intent is to guarantee that the retirement or college tuition target will be achieved or even made more likely, then such a strategy is not even approximately correct. An age-based portfolio mixing stocks and bonds can result in your missing your target by a wide margin. (We will demonstrate why this is so in Chapters 6 and 8.)

Age-based portfolios may serve to prevent inexperienced investors from making mistakes by investing in undiversified stock portfolios. However, if you want to guarantee that you reach your college goal, look to CollegeSure® CDs or I Bonds.

Free Advice

There is a lot of sound advice available these days about how to reduce the burden of paying for college, and much of it is free. You can speak to financial advisors at an intended college, or even a college near you. It's good to know what your specific state offers—in fact, it is vital. There are many new programs, but they differ from state to state.

You can also explore the Internet, which holds much information on such programs, sites that share detailed information about your specific state's programs, or more general sites like *www.collegeboard.com*, a site sponsored by a nonprofit organization dedicated to sharing timely information and trends about college, including SATs, tuition, and financial aid. Another good general site for college investment information can be found at *www.usaaedfoundation.org*, also a nonprofit site.

While touring the Internet for information specific to your needs, you may find that the sites with URLs ending in .org or .edu are more objective than those ending in .com. Still, there are numerous .com sites, such as *www.PlansForMe.com*, that hold information worth perusing.

Beware of the college investment advice you will find at the Web sites of financial firms. They want you to invest in their mutual funds or other accounts that have higher fees for them but may be too risky for you.

In this chapter, you have explored ways to invest for college education. You have looked at the special tax advantages of Section 529 plans, and the safety afforded by CollegeSure® CDs and other prepaid tuition plans. You have been warned about the risk of investing in age-based college funds that invest in stocks and bonds.

In the next chapter, you will consider an investment quite a few people make—the purchase of your home. This is one of the most important assets for almost everyone. In Chapter 5, you'll look at how to take account of this asset in your retirement planning.

5

Your Home as an Investment

In this chapter, you explore:

· How risky or safe is buying your home

· Your home as a retirement asset

· How to turn your home into cash after you retire

After weeks of watching his company's stock and mutual fund returns take more ups and downs than the roller coaster ride at Six Flags Amusement Park, Mike Sanders, on the afternoon of his 52nd birthday, sat down at the dining room table with his wife, Betty, and spread out all their files and folders, right down to the checkbook for their interest-bearing checking account. The Sanders were savvy enough to know they needed to take a hard look at their financial picture, and in committed tones, they vowed that neither of them would get up from the table until they had figured out exactly how much Mike needed to retire at 62.

As commendable as that notion was, they each did get up from the table at least once—Mike to get the Pepto Bismo, and Betty to get herself a glass of wine. As they poured through the piles of paper, particularly the recent notices of declining rates on some of their investments, they looked up at each other, and Betty finally said, "We'll need to be millionaires."

Instead of being dismayed, Mike's face lit up, and he slapped his forehead. "Wait a minute. We already are millionaires."

Betty reached for the folders. "What have we overlooked?"

"The biggest investment of our lives," he said. "It was right here in front of us, and I almost forgot about it. This house."

If you are like most people, **the single most important investment you will ever make is buying your own home. Investing in your own home is very different from investing in stocks and bonds because you will live in it.** In effect, buying your own home is like prepaying your rent for many years into the future. You are both tenant and landlord.

Is Buying Your Home a Safe Investment?

Because real estate prices fluctuate, investing in your own home could be risky. That would be true if you expected to sell your home in a year or two and move. However, if you expect to stay in the same neighborhood for many years, buying your home can be a relatively safe investment.

Purchasing your home protects you against a rise in real estate prices. It also ensures that you cannot be evicted. But what if there is a decline in real estate prices in your neighborhood? **As long as your neighborhood does not turn into a slum and you still want to continue living there, a decline in real estate prices will not affect your standard of living. Since you are both landlord and tenant, what you lose as a landlord you gain as a tenant.**

In Chapter 6, you will learn why long-term investment in the stock market is not the sure thing many people think it is. On the other hand, a good case can be made that real estate as a long-term investment contains a minimal risk, even with the sometimes downturns in the home market.

The key difference between investing in stocks and investing in a home is that you live in your house. You get service from it every day. You do not live in your stock portfolio. You may never even see the stock certificates on the shares you own. In short, being a homeowner reduces the risk to your future standard of living. Buying stocks increases the risk to your future standard of living, especially as you get closer to retirement.

Your Home as a Retirement Asset

Many people spend their early working years paying off the mortgage on a house and have nothing left over to put into an

Individual Retirement Account (IRA) or other retirement saving fund. But paying off your mortgage *can be* an important component of your savings as it was for Mike and Betty Sanders. **By the time you retire, you will probably have paid off your mortgage and own your house free and clear.**

Indeed, many people plan to sell their home when they retire. With children grown and gone, their space needs are less. They can even move to a less-expensive area where housing and perhaps other living costs are lower (like John and Joan Parker had planned to do in Chapter 1).

For the Sanders, however, it was different. Mike and Betty had moved to their house in 1982 when Motorola recruited Mike. Motorola was at that time the largest tech employer in the Austin, Texas, area with 8,000 employees. The Sanders had shopped for weeks to find the home of their dreams, a three-bedroom ranch house on three waterfront lots near Mansfield Dam on Lake Travis.

It was a reasonable commute for Mike and had a great school system for their two children, Patsy and Allen. Their dock had an electric boat winch, and they were minutes away from two great golf courses. At $250,000, it seemed a bit steep at the time, but it had everything. It was a place they could not only raise their children but could enjoy all the while, and eventually retire in some day.

That is why Betty said, "Oh, Mike. I don't want to have to sell the house just so we can retire the way we want to."

"That's just it. We won't have to sell it. We can have our cake and eat it, too."

Mike recalled an article he had read not long before about reverse mortgages as a way to draw down the equity in your home while you continue living in it for as long as you live. The article pointed out that if you had no intention of leaving your house to your children when you die, it was a sensible way to maintain your financial independence in retirement.

Both the Sanders' children, Patsy and Allen, had good careers. Patsy had become an engineer like her father, and Allen was a magazine journalist. Neither lived in Austin, and so neither would want to move into their parents' house if they inherited it. Moreover, both Patsy and Allen had repeatedly told their parents to use all of their wealth for their own retirement. They had assured their parents that they could even depend on them for support in their old age. So, reasoned Mike, maybe he should look into a reverse mortgage.

Home Equity Conversion Plans

Reverse mortgages are one of two types of what are called Home Equity Conversion (HEC) plans.[1] The second type is a sale plan. If you do not care about passing the house to an heir when you die,

---

1. A good source for information about HEC plans is HUD (*www.hud.gov/offices/hsg/sfh/ hecm/hecmabou.cfm*).

then the sale plan is the most sensible choice because you can get the most income from it with the least risk.

Under a *sale plan*, an investor, usually a bank, insurance company, or group of individuals, buys your home now but allows you to continue to live in it for as long as you live. Of course, you have to sell the house at a discount of its current value, and you have certain obligations about maintaining and insuring the house. But you get money to live on, while the buyer gets the house at a bargain price and also gets to keep any appreciation on the house while you are living in it. Once you die, or move out, for example, to a nursing home, the buyer takes possession of the house.

A *reverse mortgage* is, just as you would suspect, a mortgage in reverse. In a regular mortgage, you make monthly payments (interest as well as principal) against the debt, until it is paid off. The entire value of the house, including its increased value in the usual 30 years it takes to pay off a home mortgage, becomes your equity. In a reverse mortgage, you get a lump sum or receive monthly payments against the value of your house. It is similar to taking a home equity loan to finance your child's education.

Each payment you receive plus the accrued interest on previous payments is subtracted from the value of your house, thereby reducing your equity. **Thus, with a reverse mortgage the amount you owe to the lender grows over time. When you die, the total debt, principal plus accrued interest, is paid off, and your heirs receive any remaining equity value.**

For example, let's say you own a house worth $500,000 with no mortgage. You are 65 years old and take out a reverse mortgage loan for $100,000 at an interest rate of 6% per year. You live to age 85 and then die peacefully in your sleep at home in your own bed. You will owe the $100,000 you borrowed plus 20 years of accrued interest, which comes to another $120,714. So at your time of death, you will owe $220,714. If the house is still worth $500,000, your remaining equity after the loan is paid will be $179,286.

The house is usually sold to repay the loan, unless an heir has the means of repaying the amount in the event the house itself is desired. The house could also be sold at any time while you are still alive if you opt to live anywhere else, for example, in a nursing home.

The chief advantage of this arrangement is that you get to stay in your own home while living off your equity. You do have to pay the same real estate taxes, maintenance, and insurance premiums as before, but you are getting full benefit of your home.

Okay, would it be better for you to take out a regular home equity loan? Home equity loans require you to start making payments soon after you receive the loan. The lender does not wait until you die to collect all that is owed.

The steps to obtaining a reverse mortgage include:

· Explore the idea with a lender. Most lenders have informational sessions you need to attend before you can get a reverse mortgage. You may find that your state has a publicly funded program target for lower-income residents, if that applies.

- Determine if the amount will meet your needs. You'll find that a couple tends to get a lower monthly income than a solitary homeowner because one member of a couple is likely to outlive the other. The mortgage amount will be based on the age, value (including location), and the maximum amount available under the specific loan program.

- Explore the various types of loans. There may be several to choose from (at this time, of the 100,000 or so people who have obtained reverse mortgages, most are from the West and Northeast, where property values tend to be higher than in the rest of the nation, and most are women of approximately 75 years old).

The three basic types of reverse mortgage loans are:

- **Federal Housing Administration (FHA) insured**—With this, you won't have to repay your loan as long as you live in the house, even if your payments plus interest are more than its market value. The interest rate is adjustable, and you can choose from more payment options, such as a lump sum, monthly payments, or line of credit.[2]

---

2. A line of credit is not allowed in Texas.

- **Lender-insured**—With this, your loan can be greater than with the FHA reverse mortgage, and the interest rate may be fixed or variable. You don't have the lump sum option, however, but you can choose monthly payments or a line of credit. Some lender-insured plans include an annuity (*reverse annuity mortgage)* that will keep on paying if you are no longer living at home. The reverse annuity mortgage will affect your taxes, as explained below.

- **Uninsured**—With this, you have the most risk, but can obtain the largest amount. If, for any reason, your lender goes bankrupt, your payments will be in jeopardy. The interest rate is fixed, and it's closer to being like a regular loan in that your reverse mortgage is for a specified period of years. You will get the monthly payments you want, but when that time is up you must repay the loan. If that occurs, you will probably have to sell your house and move.

However, unless you're like Mike and Betty Sanders, whose children have no plans to come back and live in their house and do not need its inheritance value, you may want to keep your house if it has sentimental value to your family or wish to leave it as part of a legacy. In these cases, a reverse mortgage would not be right for you.

There are few better ways to stretch those other ailing retirement programs than getting the equity out of your home when you need it through a reverse mortgage. You should be aware of a few drawbacks, however, which include fees. There are upfront costs to obtaining a reverse mortgage. These include origination fees and insurance premiums. These may run in the area of 3–4.5%. For Mike and Betty Sanders, if their house is worth, say, an even $1 million (and it's probably worth more), that initial pop could be $30,000 to $45,000.[3] You will also be charged a monthly servicing fee, very much like the fees you pay when you take out a regular mortgage to buy a house.

The payments you receive from a reverse mortgage aren't taxable unless you go the reverse annuity mortgage route explained above. If you choose to repay the loan, you can only deduct the mortgage interest.

If you plan to move in the next few years, a reverse mortgage is probably not right for you, because you could not make back your upfront costs. But for people like Mike and Betty, whose retirement packages need a bit of a boost, and who want to stay in their present house yet need the equity they've invested in it, this is a sound consideration.

---

3. Check with Fannie Mae, the largest investor in mortgages in America, for a current range of such origination fees.

S · · · U · · · M · · · M · · · A · · · R · · · Y

In this chapter, you considered the merits of what is probably
your biggest investment, your home. You have seen how it can
be used to help you finance your desired retirement income. In
the next chapter you take a hard look at stocks. Is the common
belief that no matter how the stock market goes up and down,
long-term investment in the market is always good for
consistent gains true, or false?

6

Stocks Are Risky, Even in the Long Run

In this chapter, you explore:

· Why stocks are risky, even in the long run

· Saving and investing—risk and reward

· Simulations and real-world scenarios worth considering

Back when Sam Walton was listed as the richest man in America, according to *Forbes* magazine,[1] along came Black Monday,[2] and Walton saw his net wealth plummet by billions of dollars in a single day. A reporter who asked him what he intended to do was told by Sam that he would ride it out,

---

1. Based on his owning 39% of all Wal-Mart stock.
2. On October 19, 1987, the Dow Jones Industrial Average plunged 508.32 points, losing 22.6% of its total value.

that in the long run the stock market would correct itself and continue to steadily gain as it always had.

Most of us can't afford to lose a billion, or even a million, dollars. But we may agree with what Sam Walton said because that is the prevailing wisdom we have always heard. There is a widespread belief, reinforced by articles in magazines, in newspapers, and on investment Web sites, that history proves a diversified portfolio of stocks is not risky when held for periods longer than 10 years. In the aftermath of the recent decline in the stock market, many analysts are even advising people to increase their holdings of stocks because in the long run, they say, stocks are bound to recover and outperform other asset classes, including inflation-protected bonds.

One of the strong messages we want you to take away from this book is that **the proposition that stocks are safe in the long run is false, and one you can't afford to count on if your objective is worry-free investing.** If you already understand that stocks are risky no matter how long you plan to hold them, you can skip ahead to Chapter 7 on taking calculated risks. However, if you have the slightest doubt about stocks being risky in the long run, read on.

Saving and Investing—Risk and Reward

Let's revisit some basic concepts. The first two are the terms "saving" and "investing." *Saving* means setting aside part of your current income for future consumption. *Investing* means choosing which assets to hold.

Assume you earn $50,000 this year. You pay $5,000 in taxes, and you spend $40,000 on food, clothing, rent, health care, travel, and entertainment. The remaining $5,000 is your savings; and your *saving rate* is 10% ($5,000/$50,000).

You may choose to use the $5,000 of savings to buy stocks or I Bonds. This choice is an investment decision. If you choose I Bonds, you are making a safe investment; if you choose stocks, you are making a risky investment. If you choose to leave it in your bank account, that, too, is an investment decision.

Investing in I Bonds is safe because you know in advance what the value of your investment will be in terms of future purchasing power. Investing in stocks is risky because the future value of your stock portfolio is not known with certainty, and it may turn out to be less than what you could have had with I Bonds. If you decide to invest in stocks, you do so for the potential reward of having a greater amount of purchasing power in the future than you could have had with I Bonds.

During the heady, optimistic decade of the 1990s, the myth was born that for the long-term investor, stocks offered higher rewards with virtually no risk. In a book by a well-known financial journalist and a respected economist published in late 1999, the authors told their readers that the Dow Jones Industrial Average was likely to rise from 11,000 to 36,000 within the foreseeable future. No wonder that ordinary people planning for retirement (like John and Joan Parker) or for their children's college education (like the Sullivan family) were swept up in this euphoria!

The objective of this book is not to convince you to avoid stocks altogether. Rather it is to equip you with an understanding of the true risks and rewards you face in choosing your investment portfolio. The objective is to steer you toward a more worry-free path.

An Objective View

The myth that investing in stocks is safe in the long run rests on a misinterpretation of the history of stock market returns in the United States. Figure 6.1 is usually shown to support this myth. It shows that an investor would have done far better investing in stocks back in 1926 rather than in bonds or in bills. The inflation-adjusted real rate of return on stocks for the 75-year period 1926–2000 was 9.3% per year, far more than the rates of return on bonds and on money market instruments.

A sum of $100 invested in a diversified portfolio consisting of all stocks listed on the New York Stock Exchange (NYSE) in January 1926 would have increased in value to almost $200,000 (the upper line in the chart). This assumes that all dividends received are reinvested. After adjusting for inflation over the same 75 years, you see that the portfolio's value in terms of constant purchasing power increased far less—only one-tenth as much to $20,000. However, that is far more than you would have earned

Real Cumulative Return Indexes

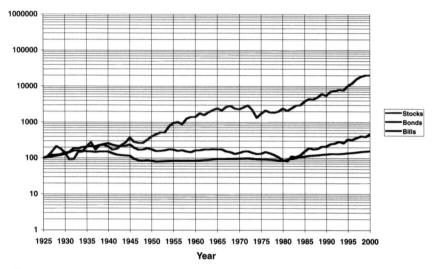

Figure 6.1
Performance of stocks, bonds, and bills
1926–2000.

by investing in bonds. At an inflation-adjusted (real) interest rate of 3% per year, $100 invested in bonds would have grown to only $918. What can you validly infer from this information?

Beware the wisdom of hindsight! Anyone can score 100% accuracy when predicting the past. Disraeli[3] once said that there are lies, damn lies, and statistics. That saying applies in this case.

Even if you take 9.3% to be the *expected* rate of return on stocks over the long term in the future, the actual rate of return over any specific period can turn out to be very different. Consider the

---

3. A mid-19th Century British Prime Minister.

year-by-year stock returns for the same period, 1926–2000 (shown in Figure 6.2).

Over the period 1926–2000, the annual rate of return fluctuated unpredictably, that is, *randomly*, around the long-term average. The standard deviation, a measure of the *volatility* of annual stock returns, was 20.3%. Think of standard deviation as the shallows and deeps of a stream you wish to cross. If the average depth is four feet, and you know the shallows don't reach your ankles, you can count on the stream being over your head at some point. **If you are not a good swimmer, you can easily drown in a stream whose average depth is four feet.**

Real Stock Returns: 1926–2000

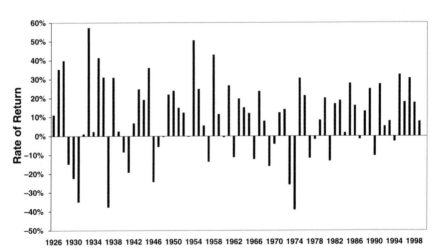

Figure 6.2
Real annual stock returns
1926–2000.

The pattern of annual rates of return shown in Figure 6.2 is typical of a series of data that is random. With such a pattern, **you can never count on the value of your stock portfolio being sufficient to cover what you absolutely need at any point in the future.** There is always a chance that when you reach retirement age or your child reaches college age, your stock portfolio will fall far short of what you planned. **Following an age-based strategy of automatically switching from stocks to bonds or bills as you approach your target date does not solve this problem because you may just be locking in a loss rather than a gain. The only genuine worry-free solution is to lock in your target at the outset by investing in default-free inflation-protected bonds that match your needs in terms of timing and amount.**

Why Are Stocks Risky?

Stocks are risky because each share of stock is a part ownership in a business. Business is risky because every business has to deal with changing customer tastes, competition, unexpected changes in the economy, and many other factors that are often unpredictable. **Many businesses, even very large businesses, fail each year. If you own shares in one of those businesses, you lose.**

As those who owned shares in Polaroid, Enron, WorldCom, etc., learned, even owning stocks in a large company with a well-known brand name and a reputation for good management is risky. Even *all* firms in an industry can lose money over long periods, as proven by the history of the airlines.

That is why experts recommend diversifying your investment in stocks across many firms in different industries. While diversification reduces your exposure to the risk of a particular company, it does not reduce your exposure to the risk of the stock market as a whole. There are many factors, such as the risk of a general business downturn, that affect the value of all stocks.

Stock prices, according to finance professors who have studied them, tend to move randomly around a trend, so predicting them is like predicting the outcome of tossing dice. Even though you may remember the sequence of the past throws, that knowledge will not help you predict the outcome of the next toss.

Figure 6.3
Stock returns behave in the same random fashion as dice throws.

The reason stock returns behave in this random fashion is that the price of a stock reflects the expectations of millions of investors about the future earnings and price performance of the underlying firms. Those expectations change in response to new information—news about technological discoveries and inventions, changes in consumer buying patterns, announcements of mergers or acquisitions, a change in government regulations.

New information of this sort arrives unpredictably over time (though it seems to be happening faster and faster with our heightened media). **It does not matter whether investor expectations change in a rational way, as economists of the "efficient markets" school believe, or as the result of mass psychology as "behavioral" economists believe, the result is the same—stock prices will fluctuate randomly.**

Investment advisors who promote stocks for the long run acknowledge that investing in stocks is risky, but claim that the risk of owning stocks declines the longer you hold them. Over the long term, they say, stocks are no more risky than bonds, and far more rewarding. They point to the historical returns of stock investing to support this claim.

Misleading Statistics

To understand why the risk of stocks does *not* decline as the time horizon gets longer, let's consider the outcomes of a series of tosses of dice. Each year, you toss the dice. The outcome on each toss has an expected or probable value (*mean*) of 7. But it could be any number between 2 and 12. Figure 6.4 shows the probability of each of the possible outcomes.

Here you can see in clear hard data that the number that will occur most is 7. If you were to toss the same pair of dice for days, weeks, or even years, the number that would turn up most often will be 7.

Does that make 7 a sure thing?

No, it just means that it will have the highest frequency of occurring. There will also be many outcomes of 6, 8, 5, 9, etc. You can

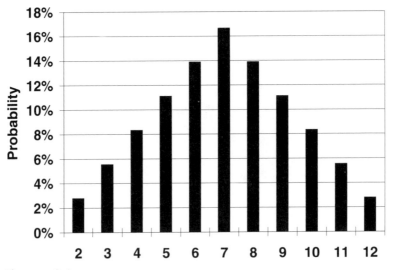

Figure 6.4
Probability distribution outcome of
random tosses of dice.

even have a run of 10 tosses without a single outcome greater than 6. That is the nature of chance.

The rational proposition that the stock market has an *expected* rate of return of 9.3% per year is similar to the fact that the *expected* outcome on each roll of the dice is 7. As with dice, it is quite possible that there will be a run of 10 years in which the stock market earns far less than 9.3% per year.

Take a look at Figure 6.5, which shows how 75 random rolls of a pair of dice might turn out. We simulated these results by actually tossing a pair of dice 75 consecutive times and recording the outcomes.

This random pattern is strikingly similar to the pattern you see for stock returns in Figure 6.2. But, let's put aside the dice and simulate stock returns in much the same way.

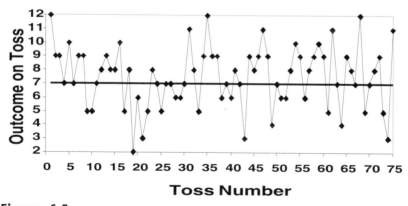

Figure 6.5
Simulated outcome pattern of 75
tosses of a pair of dice.

Simulating Stock Returns

Analysts often perform simulations to get a picture of the range of possible outcomes for stock market portfolios. Figure 6.6 is an example. It shows the outcomes of three different simulation runs of 30 years.

As a benchmark for comparison, we show the real wealth accumulation for an investor earning a risk-free interest rate of 3% per year. At the end of 30 years, he or she would have $243. Note that in the first two simulation runs the stock portfolio has a final value well in excess of $243: In run 1, the final value is about $750, and in run 3, it is about $2,000. However, in run 2, the portfolio's final value is only $52—about half of what you started with and less than a quarter of what you would have had by investing in I Bonds.

When we simulate future scenarios, we see that very bad outcomes can occur for long-time horizons. When the time comes to use the money you have been investing, the only thing that will matter to you is the path of your *own* portfolio's value. Because it could turn out to be like the one depicted in simulation run 2 in Figure 6.6, we say that stocks are risky even in the long run.

The Effect of Periodic Withdrawals

In the previous section, you examined the risk of investing a sum of money in a diversified portfolio of stocks for 30 years and not touching it during the entire period, instead reinvesting any cash

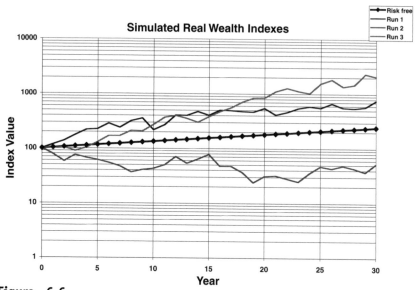

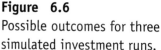

Figure 6.6

Possible outcomes for three
simulated investment runs.

dividends received in the stock market. You saw that, because of
the random character of stock market returns, you might wind up
with very little at the end of 30 years. But the sequence of rates of
returns does not affect the final outcome.

To see why the sequence of rates of return does *not* matter when
there are no withdrawals of money, consider an investment of
$100 with the following three sequences over a three-year period:

Sequence 1: You gain 5%, then lose 10%, then gain 20%.

Sequence 2: You lose 10%, then gain 5%, then gain 20%.

Sequence 3: You gain 20%, then gain 5%, then lose 10%.

In each case, you wind up with the same amount of money at the end of the three years: $113.40. The sequence does not matter.

However, if you withdraw money during the 30-year period, the sequence of rates of return matters very much. This becomes critical during your retirement, when you are living on the money you withdraw from your accumulated savings.

For example, suppose you plan to save a total of $1 million, expect to live for 20 years after retirement, and assume an average rate of return of 10% per year. You calculate the annual retirement income you can withdraw to be $117,496 per year. Table 6.1 shows that by withdrawing this amount at the end of each year, you will precisely exhaust your original fund in 20 years—*provided that you earn 10% in each and every year.*

Table 6.1 Optimal Annual Retirement Income for 20 Years After Retirement

Year	Rate of Return	Amount in Fund	Interest Earned	Amount Withdrawn
1	10%	$1,000,000	$100,000	$117,460
2	10%	$982,540	$98,254	$117,460
3	10%	$963,335	$96,333	$117,460
4	10%	$942,209	$94,221	$117,460
5	10%	$918,970	$91,897	$117,460

Table 6.1   Optimal Annual Retirement Income for 20 Years
After Retirement (Continued)

Year	Rate of Return	Amount in Fund	Interest Earned	Amount Withdrawn
6	10%	$893,407	$89,341	$117,460
7	10%	$865,288	$86,529	$117,460
8	10%	$834,358	$83,436	$117,460
9	10%	$800,334	$80,033	$117,460
10	10%	$762,907	$76,291	$117,460
11	10%	$721,739	$72,174	$117,460
12	10%	$676,453	$67,645	$117,460
13	10%	$626,638	$62,664	$117,460
14	10%	$571,843	$57,184	$117,460
15	10%	$511,567	$51,157	$117,460
16	10%	$445,264	$44,526	$117,460
17	10%	$372,331	$37,233	$117,460
18	10%	$292,105	$29,210	$117,460
19	10%	$203,856	$20,386	$117,460
20	10%	$106,781	$10,678	$117,460
21		$0	$0	

Suppose your rate of return varies over the 20 years. Even if the average is 10% per year, it makes a big difference whether the higher-than-average returns occur early or late in the 20-year span. What if during the first 10 years your rate of return is below average and during the last 10 years it is above average?

You may not make it past the tenth year. For example, suppose the rate of return is 0% in the first 10 years, and 20% per year in the last 10 years. You start out with $1 million and withdraw $117,460 per year. This situation is shown in Table 6.2 and depicted in Figure 6.7. Since your fund would earn no interest at all during the first half of the period, you would completely run out of money by the ninth year.

Table 6.2   Retirement Fund When Rate of Return During First 10 Years Is 0%

Year	Rate of Return	Amount in Fund	Interest Earned	Amount Withdrawn at End of Year
1	0	$1,000,000	$0	$117,460
2	0	$882,540	$0	$117,460
3	0	$765,081	$0	$117,460
4	0	$647,621	$0	$117,460
5	0	$530,162	$0	$117,460
6	0	$412,702	$0	$117,460

Table 6.2 Retirement Fund When Rate of Return During First 10 Years Is 0% (Continued)

Year	Rate of Return	Amount in Fund	Interest Earned	Amount Withdrawn at End of Year
7	0	$295,242	$0	$117,460
8	0	$177,783	$0	$117,460
9	0	$60,323	$0	$117,460
10	0	-$57,137	$0	$117,460

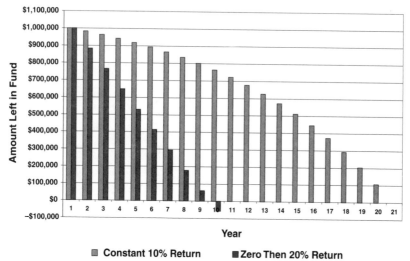

Figure 6.7
How long $1 million will last.

This is not merely a far-fetched hypothetical situation. Consider a real-world example. Suppose you had retired in January 1973 with a retirement fund of $1 million. The average rate of return on a value-weighted portfolio of all stocks on the NYSE during the 20 years starting in 1973 was a healthy 12.78% per year. Suppose you were conservative and assumed only a 10% rate of return. You therefore planned to take out $117,460 each year.

The pattern of actual annual returns and remaining funds is shown in Table 6.3 and depicted in Figure 6.8. Keep in mind we're not talking about simulation or expectations now. We're discussing what really happened when it mattered.

Table 6.3 Actual Values for Retiree Starting in 1973

Year	Rate of Return	Amount in Fund	Return on Investment	Amount Before Withdrawl	Amount Withdrawn
1973	-14.75%	$1,000,000	-$147,500	$852,500	$117,460
1974	-26.40%	$735,040	-$194,051	$540,990	$117,460
1975	37.26%	$423,530	$157,807	$581,337	$117,460
1976	23.98%	$463,878	$111,238	$575,116	$117,460
1977	-7.26%	$457,656	-$33,226	$424,430	$117,460
1978	6.50%	$306,971	$19,953	$326,924	$117,460
1979	18.77%	$209,464	$39,316	$248,780	$117,460

Table 6.3   Actual Values for Retiree Starting in 1973

Year	Rate of Return	Amount in Fund	Return on Investment	Amount Before Withdrawl	Amount Withdrawn
1980	32.48%	$131,321	$42,653	$173,974	$117,460
1981	-4.98%	$56,514	-$2,814	$53,700	$117,460
1982	22.09%	-$63,760	-$14,085	-$77,844	$117,460

Take a detailed look at what would have happened. In 1973, the stock market declined 14.75%, so at the end of the year, you

Retiree Who Started in 1973

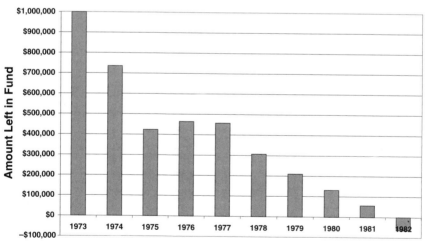

Figure 6.8
Retiree who started in 1973.

would have had only $852,500. After you take out your $117,460, you would have had $735,040 left in the fund. In 1974, the market drops an additional 26.5%, dropping your account balance to $540,990. At the end of 1974, you again take out $117,460, leaving you a new account balance of $423,530. In other words, by the end of 1974, you have less than half of your original $1,000,000 left, even though you only took out a total of $234,920.

In 1975, the market gains 37.2%, lifting your balance to $581,337. Again you withdraw your $117,460, leaving a balance of $463,878. In 1976, the market climbs 23.8%, raising your balance to $575,116, from which you again take your $117,460, leaving a balance of $457,656. The next year, 1977, is a bad year with a market return of –7.2%. Your account balance declines to $424,430, from which you withdraw your $117,460 for living expenses, and so on. By the time you reach 1981, you have only $56,514 left in the fund. That year your return is –4.98%, and you can no longer take your $117,460 to live on.

Thus, you can see that even though *on average* from 1973 through 1992, the market returned a rate of return of 11.3% per year, and you had been counting on only 10% per year in your withdrawal plan, you have run out of money before the tenth year.

Japan's Stock Market Crash—An Example to Remember

To reinforce the lesson that stocks are risky even in the long run, consider what happened in Japan. During the 1970s and especially the 1980s, many prominent analysts viewed Japan as a major economic challenger to the United States, and the prices of Japanese stocks soared. The Nikkei 225 reached its peak of just over 40,000 in 1989. It then plunged, and despite temporary recoveries, as of this writing, it was 8,879. What happened to stocks in Japan can happen in the United States, too.

In this chapter, you learned that the supposition that stocks are safe in the long run is false. You explored the random nature of the stock market and how history reveals that stock returns are best characterized as a random process over time.

When future scenarios and actual 10-year periods in the past, both in the United States and in Japan, were simulated, you saw that very bad outcomes can occur for long-time horizons.

In the next chapter, you will look at if and when it is appropriate for you to take calculated risks.

7

Taking Calculated Risks in the Stock Market

In this chapter, you explore:

· Whether you should invest in the stock market

· If you should invest in the company where you work

· New ways to participate in stock market gains

O ur goal has been to show you how to invest in a way that will leave you worry-free. We have suggested that you focus first on those goals that are *essential* for you to reach—retirement and your kids' college education— and that you invest enough in I Bonds and other safe investments to guarantee that you will not fall short. You have seen that every dollar you save for these essential goals can be invested in instruments that are sure to beat inflation.

If you have enough invested safely so that you are not worried about achieving your essential goals, then you could consider taking some investment risks. Ask yourself: How much can I afford to lose without starting to worry? **Put at risk only as much money as you feel you can afford to lose.**

In this chapter, we discuss the key factors for you to consider in deciding how much of your money to invest in the stock market. We also describe how to get extra bang for your buck in terms of potential gains by using options on stocks and on stock indexes.

Who Should Invest in Stocks?

In Chapter 1, you met John Parker, who was in his sixties when he realized that he and his wife, Joan, needed to take a hard second look at their retirement plans. At the beginning of 2002, the Parkers accepted that they had to delay retirement, probably to at least age 65. They also accepted that they would have to save more money and invest it safely in inflation-protected securities.

John was concerned that he would regret taking the new safe strategy should the stock market come roaring back in the next year or two. He suspected he would regret not sharing in any gains a new bull market might deliver, especially if those gains would have allowed him to retire earlier. He wondered how he could avoid that sense of regret without further endangering his retirement income by remaining invested in stocks

The conventional wisdom says that the younger you are, the more you should invest in stocks. The rule of thumb is that the proportion to invest in stocks should be 100 minus your age. Is the conventional wisdom right?

The conventional wisdom is too simplistic.

First and foremost, how much you invest in stocks should depend on the market risks you are already exposed to through your business or profession. To understand why, let's consider an extreme case. Jim Gooding and his wife, Doris, live in Rochester, New York. They both work for Kodak, which is the major employer in Rochester. Their main assets are their house and their profit-sharing plan at Kodak. How much of their portfolio should they then invest in Kodak stock?

The answer is not one red cent! The reason is the Goodings are already heavily exposed to the risk of Kodak. If Kodak profits decline because a competitor such as Fuji unexpectedly develops a cheaper, better type of film, not only would Kodak's stock price fall, but both of the Goodings could lose their jobs.

They might have to sell their house and move from Rochester. Because lots of other Kodak employees could very well be selling their homes at the same time, they would probably have to take a loss on the value of their house.

What the Goodings really need is insurance against a decline in Kodak's stock price, not more exposure to it through their profit-sharing plan.

Before deciding how to invest in stocks, you should carefully consider your existing risk exposure. You may not be exposed to a single stock the way the Goodings are, but you probably are exposed to the level of stock prices as whole.

The level of stock prices and the health of the economy are closely connected. Most people employed in the private sector face income risk if the stock market suffers a decline. Such declines can lead to recessions, with massive layoffs. You could be one of those layoffs. How stable is the income from your job? Civil servants and tenured professors may face relatively little risk, but how about you?

Your market-risk exposure may actually be greater when you are young than when you are old. For example, suppose that after graduating from college you decide to become an entrepreneur and start your own business. You devote all of your time and energy to building a successful new business venture. That means that your welfare depends very much on the state of the economy and the stock market. Your portfolio of investments—if you have one besides your investment in your own business—should surely be invested mostly in safe assets like Treasury Inflation-Protected Securities (TIPS) or IBonds.

Later in life, if you are successful, you may decide to sell your business. At that point, depending on your age and how much wealth you have, you may want to change the asset mix in your investment portfolio and invest more heavily in stocks. If you have more than enough assets to guarantee a comfortable

retirement, you certainly could invest the extra money in stocks.

Thus, your age profile of stock market investing would be very different from the conventional wisdom's rule of thumb—you would want to hold safe assets when young and switch part of your investments to stocks as you grow older. As you approach retirement, if you have only enough wealth to provide income for yourself and your spouse, you may want to reduce your stock holdings again and switch back to safer assets such as inflation-protected annuities.

Protecting Your Principal

One approach to taking risks that might leave you free of worry is to make sure that you get back at least your original principal. You can do this by investing enough in safe assets to cover your principal and invest the rest in risky assets. For example, suppose you have $100,000 in your investment fund and want to be sure that a year from now you will have at least that much. Suppose also that a one-year FDIC-insured bank Certificate of Deposit (CD) is paying an interest rate of 3%. You need only invest $97,087.38—$100,000/1.03—in a CD to have it grow to $100,000 in a year.

That leaves $2,912.62 to invest in something risky, like stocks. You might decide to buy shares of a promising biotech company that you have been researching, or you might invest in a broadly diversified mutual fund that holds the S&P 500. You might even take a flier on stock options, which we discuss next.

Call Options

Call options can be used as alternatives to stock investments, giving you more bang for the buck. A *call option* gives you the right to buy the underlying stock. It has a *strike price* (the price at which you can buy the stock) and an expiration date. Buying a call option is like making a security deposit on a house when you sign a purchase agreement. If you fail to buy the house by a specified date, you lose your deposit and the house is put back on the market.

Likewise, when you buy a call option you are, in effect, putting down a nonrefundable deposit for the right to buy a stock from the seller at an agreed-upon price (the strike price) by an agreed-upon date. If the price of the stock rises above the market price, you buy the stock at the strike price and have an immediate gain. If it does not, you allow the option to expire and lose your deposit.

For example, consider a call option on XYZ stock that has a strike price of $100 per share and a one-year maturity. Currently, the price of XYZ stock is $100. The cost of the XYZ option might be $10. If a year from now the price of XYZ stock is $120, you will exercise your option. You will pay $100 for the stock that is worth $120, so you will have a profit of $10 on your investment of $10 in the option. That is a profit of 100% of your investment in the option.

Compared to investing in XYZ stock, buying an XYZ option gives you more bang for your buck because it costs a fraction of the price of the stock, yet it can go up in value by the same amount. Had you invested $100 in a share of XYZ stock, your profit would be $20. But for the same $100 you could buy options on 10 shares and make a profit of $100 if the stock price rises to $120. You get five times the upside gain per dollar invested.

That is the good news about options. **The bad news about options is that if the stock price does not go up, the option expires and is worthless; you lose 100% of your investment.** If you invest in the stock and it does not go up, you gain nothing and you lose nothing and are left with stock that is still probably worth something.

Listed call options on individual stocks have been available since 1973 when the Chicago Board Options Exchange first opened. Long-Term Equity Anticipation Securities (LEAPS) are options with expiration dates of up to three years from the date they are first listed.

Buying a call option on the S&P 500 stock index is equivalent to buying call options on shares of a stock whose price performance matches the performance of the index. The difference is that **when you invest in the options instead of the stock you forego any cash dividends paid. In addition, the options have an expiration date while the stocks do not.**

To illustrate how you make or lose money by investing in call options, consider an investment in a single option that gives you the right to buy a share of S&P 500 stock. For simplicity, assume that the price of each share of the underlying stock is currently $100. You select an option with the longest possible maturity date, three years, and you plan to hold the option until its expiration date. You can choose from an array of different strike prices, so you choose a strike price equal to what you think the dollar value of the index will be if it grows at the same rate as inflation, say, 3% per year. That way you will at least protect the purchasing power of your investment.

The strike price in our example is:

$$\$100 \times 1.03 \times 1.03 \times 1.03 = \$109.27$$

Say the price of the call option is $13.80. That is the price the seller of the option is demanding for the transaction.

At the expiration date, three years from now, if the S&P 500 index is less than the option's strike price of $109.27, your option expires worthless. You will have lost your entire investment of $13.80. However, if the index is greater than $109.27, the seller of the option must pay you the difference between the index value and 109.27. For example, if the index has risen to $150, then you receive $40.73 (the difference between $150 and $109.27). In other words, you would get back almost three times what you paid for the option. You would make a profit of 195% on your investment of $13.80:

$$\textit{Your profit} = \$40.73 - \$13.80 = \$26.93$$

Your rate of return = 100 x $26.93/$13.80 = 195%

Note that this rate of return is earned over a three-year period. It is not annualized. The annualized rate of return is 24.9%. That is, if you invested $13.80 at 24.9% per year it would grow to $26.93.

REVIEW QUESTION

If the index value at the expiration date is $130 instead of $150, what would be your profit? What would be your rate of return?

You will receive in cash $20.73, the difference between the $130 value of the index and the strike price of $109.27.

Your profit = $20.73 – $13.80 = $6.93
Your rate of return = 100 x $6.93/$13.80 = 50%

That's a 14.5% annualized rate of return.

Combining Bonds with Stock Options

Now consider how you can combine options with bonds to participate in market gains while protecting your principal. Again, assume you have $100,000 to invest, and you think that three years from now the stock market may be much higher than it is today. Assume that the interest rate is 3% per year. To guarantee your $100,000 principal, you would need to invest only $91,514 in inflation-protected bonds. To see this, verify that by investing this amount to earn a compound real rate of interest of 3% per year will result in your having $100,000 in three years' time:

$$\$91,514 \times 1.03 \times 1.03 \times 1.03 = \$100,000$$

You invest the rest of your $100,000—$8,486—in LEAPS on the S&P 500 index that expire three years from now. As in the previous example, assume that the price of each share of the underlying S&P stock is $100 and that you choose an option with a strike price of $109.27. As before, say that the price of each option is $13.80.

How many of these options can you buy with your $8,486? The answer is $8,486/$13.8, which is roughly 615.

Let's analyze how your $100,000 investment in a portfolio of inflation-protected bonds and S&P 500 call options performs compared to $100,000 invested in S&P 500 shares. This is shown in Figure 7.1 and Table 7.1.

The horizontal axis in Figure 7.1 measures the value of the index when the options expire three years from now and the vertical axis the value of your total investment—bonds plus cash from the options. For example, if you invest all of your money in shares in an S&P 500 index fund, and at the end of three years the value of the index is only 50, then the value of your portfolio would be only $50,000. This is shown by the dotted line in Figure 7.1. However, if the value of the index is 200 (on the bottom axis), then the value of an all-stock portfolio would be $200. When the portfolio is a combination of inflation-protected bonds and call options, the outlook changes. The value of the portfolio never falls below $100,000. This is shown by the solid line.

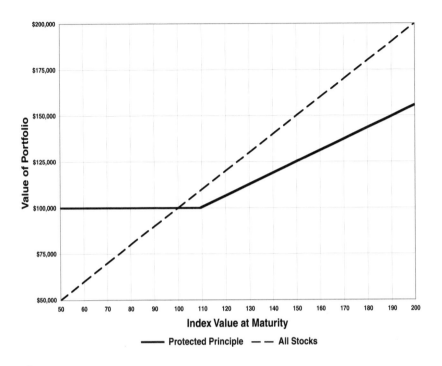

Figure 7.1
Projected values of portfolios at
maturity.

Table 7.1 Projected Values of Portfolios at Maturity

Index Value at Maturity	Value of Protected Principal Portfolio	Value of All Stock Portfolio
50	$100,000	$50,000
70	$100,000	$70,000
90	$100,000	$90,000

Table 7.1   Projected Values of Portfolios at Maturity (Continued)

Index Value at Maturity	Value of Protected Principal Portfolio	Value of All Stock Portfolio
100	$100,000	$100,000
110	$100,449	$110,000
130	$112,749	$130,000
150	$125,049	$150,000
170	$137,349	$170,000
190	$149,649	$190,000
200	$155,799	$200,000

Note the kink in the curve at 109.27. If the S&P 500 is less than 109.27 at the end of three years, the options expire worthless, and your investment portfolio will be worth $100,000—the inflation-adjusted value of the bonds. But if the index has risen above 109.27, your portfolio rises in value by $6.15 for every $10 increase in the price of the index.

Let's say that the index increases to 150. Each of your 615 options entitles you to buy a share of S&P 500 stock at $109.27. Then the value of the protected principal portfolio will be $125,049. While that is less than the $150,000 the portfolio would have been worth had it been invested entirely in shares of the S&P 500, it gains roughly half of the full $50,000 gain. On the other hand, if the index falls to 50, the protected portfolio will be worth $100,000 rather than the $50,000 you would have had.

REVIEW QUESTION

Suppose that the cost of each option in our example were $20 instead of $13.80. How many options could you buy with your $8,486, and how would that affect your participation in market gains?

The number of options you could buy would be $8,486/$20, which is roughly 424 instead of 615. So, if the S&P 500 index rises from 100 to 150, your portfolio would be worth only $117,270, instead of $125,049.

One strategy that John Parker might adopt is to invest 10% of his retirement assets in index call options to participate in any market recovery, while keeping 90% of his assets invested safely in TIPS. That way he can preserve the bulk of his retirement assets and earn a small real return on them from the TIPS, while sharing in any market recovery. This might allow him to retire a little earlier, and it might relieve any pangs of regret from being heavily in TIPS if the stock market should surge.

However, as noted, this approach, while a low-risk one compared to investing all of your money in the stock market, is not risk-free. If the stock market does not recover, John would lose the premium he paid for his options each time they expire worthless. Over time, that can add up.

Convertible Bonds

Convertible bonds are hybrid investments that combine the features of corporate bonds and stocks. Like regular corporate bonds, they have a fixed maturity and pay a promised rate of interest. However, they are also convertible into a fixed number of shares of the issuing company's common stock, at the option of the bondholder. For example, say XYZ issues a 30-year bond with a face value of $1,000 that is convertible into 10 shares of XYZ common stock. The promised interest rate is 2.5% per year.

Say the price of XYZ stock is $50 per share. An investor who bought such a bond would not even consider converting his or her bonds into stocks unless its conversion value exceeded its value as a bond. Thus, if the price of the stock rose to $100 per share and the price of the bond were $1,000, it would be at break even—the bond's price would equal what the bondholder could receive if he or she converted it into 10 shares of stock and sold the stock at $100 per share.

Buying an XYZ convertible bond is similar to buying a straight XYZ bond plus 10 call options on XYZ stock with an exercise price equal to the bond's price. But it differs from the strategy of investing in TIPS plus call options in several important ways.

First, with the XYZ convertible bond you face the risk of default if XYZ company goes bankrupt. Second, the XYZ convertible bond can only be converted into XYZ stock. With the TIPS plus call options strategy, you can buy call options on any stocks or indexes you want.

Principal-Protected Equity-Participation Notes

Some investment firms sell *principal-protected equity-participation notes* that have the same features as the portfolio we have created by combining bonds and index options. For example, Merrill Lynch sells such securities as Market-Index Target Term Securities (MITTS). However, there are several important differences:

· Our bonds plus index calls strategy is inflation-protected.

· Our protected portfolio is free of default risk, while MITTS and other such securities are only as safe as the firm that issues them.

· The principal-protected securities (like MITTS) may be overpriced relative to the bonds plus index calls strategy. That's because the firms selling such products charge a fee for providing the principal protection. The fee may be explicit or may take the form of the company keeping a very large share of any market gain.

ING offers a series of mutual funds, which it calls the Principal Protection Funds, that do the same thing. The company does not guarantee any investment return, only that you will get your principal back. If the stock market goes up, you will get the return on the fixed-income securities, plus part of the stock market's gain. ING's approach is to vary the amount of stocks and bonds in the mutual funds over a five-year period. It buys 400 to 450 of the stocks in the S&P 500 index, attempting to get a little better return on those stocks than the index alone would give by buying different amounts than are in the index.

Most investors should use TIPS and I Bonds alone. You should not invest in equity-linked securities or stock index options without the help of an investment professional. Such a professional can guide you through the intricacies of buying such unusual investment vehicles, including the required paperwork. While it may be possible to invest in stocks through the Internet without the guidance of a financial professional, it is not advisable for most people. Flying solo, with more sophisticated investments, is even less advisable.

After considering the above alternatives, John Parker decided that an options strategy was not appropriate for him, for the same reasons putting a deposit on a North Carolina home wasn't his best choice. He worried that the premiums from expiring unexercised call options would eat into his savings. Those expiring premiums were a cost that could mount up if the stock market failed to recover, because the options would never reach the strike price.

Instead, he decided to explore the use of equity-linked securities and ING's Principal Protection Funds. They might relieve his concern about lost opportunity regret if the market should come storming back. He simply had to choose among the various products to see which best suited his situation. He decided to talk to his financial advisor about it.

In this chapter, you explored how much risk you can tolerate as an investor. You also looked at the assumption that the young can tolerate more risk. In truth, it depends on your situation. In some cases, the opposite may be true. You also looked at how you can increase your upside potential while limiting your downside risk. In the next chapter, you consider some pitfalls of investing and how to avoid them.

8

Investment Pitfalls and How to Avoid Them

In this chapter, you explore:

- How doing your own investing requires clear vision
- Common errors of perception and myths about investing
- The role of chance—how investing is no game

t pays for you to become informed about investing. Remember the old saying that a fool and his money are soon parted. **Relatively few people have the training, temperament, and discipline needed to correctly analyze the vast amounts of investment information available in books, magazines, and on the Internet. Those who do have the training are not inclined to give you sound advice for free.**

The situation is similar to the one you face with medical care. Most of us look to doctors and nurses to guide our choices about health maintenance and treatments for illnesses. Yet when it comes to investing our money, we are encouraged to handle it on our own. Like surgery, investing money properly is a complex process, requiring much knowledge and years of training.

No one would imagine that patients could perform surgery to remove their own appendix after reading an explanation in a brochure published by a surgical equipment company. Why should we expect people to choose an appropriate mix of stocks, bonds, and cash after reading a brochure published by a securities firm? Some people are likely to make serious mistakes. Even professionals who have the training and discipline still make mistakes and often underperform the stock market indexes.

The educational materials distributed to customers by financial service firms seek to present a different, more favorable impression of stock investing. Customers are led to believe that stocks are not risky in the long run. Online asset allocation tools are heavily biased toward equity investment.

Rarely is mention made of truly safe long-term investments such as government inflation-protected bonds and real annuities. Brokerage firms want you to buy and sell stocks to generate trading commissions for them. That's how they make money. Mutual fund companies want you to buy mutual fund shares, especially of stock funds, because they generate high management fees.

Chapter 8
Investment Pitfalls and How to Avoid Them

Many pitfalls await you if you are an unwary investor. **Some arise because of the way we humans perceive random events.**

For example, you have probably met someone like Gladys Fitzgerald. Gladys likes to play the slot machines at casinos, and she will sit feeding coins into the same machine for hours on end. Gladys is convinced that the longer a slot machine goes without making a big payoff, the more likely it is the machine will pay off on the next pull, or the one after it, and the larger the payoff is likely to be. This is called **the gambler's myth—believing that a good outcome must follow a string of bad ones.**

On the other hand, if Gladys gets a few decent-sized payoffs from her chosen slot machine, she assumes it's a lucky machine and will stick with that machine for hours. She sees no conflict between these two ideas. In fact, both ideas are equally false. Slot machines are designed to pay off randomly. There is no pattern to when they pay off, and every pull on every machine is equally likely (or unlikely) to produce a payoff.

Investors also are prone to errors of perception like this. In this chapter, you will explore some of the major pitfalls that investors face and how you can avoid them. Some of the myths that you will explore are actually believed to be true by professional financial planners and investment advisors.

Here are six myths about investing:

Myth 1: It is easy to beat stock market professionals at their own game.

Myth 2: You can identify the best money managers by looking at their track records.

Myth 3: Stocks are not risky in the long run.

Myth 4: Stocks are the best hedge against inflation.

Myth 5: Dollar cost averaging improves your risk-reward tradeoff.

Myth 6: An age-based portfolio strategy is the best way to secure your lifecycle saving targets.

Myth 1: It Is Easy to Beat Stock Market Professionals at Their Own Game

The first myth is the belief that with a little effort you can beat the market—that is, earn a higher return by picking your own stocks or relying on the advice of your broker than you can earn by investing in a broad-based index fund. Hundreds (if not thousands) of books have been written telling you how to beat the market. Many radio and television shows are devoted to interviewing company executives, financial analysts, and portfolio managers who offer their advice to amateur stock pickers.

These books and shows may have great entertainment value, but they are unlikely to improve your chances of beating a simple low-cost strategy of investing in stock market index funds. **Trying to beat the market can cost you. It can lead you to take excessive risk or to trade your stocks too often.**

Chapter 8
Investment Pitfalls and How to Avoid Them

Taking too much risk can really hurt your finances if the stock market falls because higher risk stocks will plunge faster than the market as a whole. Trading your stocks too often will chew up a good part of any returns you may earn on your investments. It is very difficult to consistently beat the market average for several reasons.

First, the market price for each stock represents a market consensus view of thousands of investors. Many of these investors, or their money managers, have closely studied the company to determine its likely future sales and earnings growth rates. Because so many people are examining each company, it's very difficult for any one investor, or group of investors, to gain an information advantage in time to act on it and profit from it before everyone else knows it and the market adjusts.

Scholars who have used rigorous scientific procedures to analyze the data say the stock market is very quick to adjust to new information. Easy profit opportunities do not last for long. With diligent effort you may occasionally get a jump on the market, but it is rare. Even professional money managers have difficulty beating the market averages consistently over the long run. An amateur investor is competing with the professionals.

Second, it is very difficult to consistently beat the market because of the cost of buying and selling shares. Index funds, which invest in the stocks tracked by market indexes, minimize these costs. They buy and sell only when a stock is dropped or added to the fund, or to allow investors to cash out or buy into the fund.

Active managers and investors trying to outperform the average market return buy and sell shares frequently. Every time you buy or sell a stock, you pay a commission. If you buy and sell frequently, these costs can be significant. If you invest through a mutual fund, you pay these costs through the management fee. These costs hurt performance.

In addition to the costs of trading, there is the cost of research. Actively managed funds require research departments to figure out which stocks to buy and sell—the better the training of the staff, the higher the cost. Even if the research department does a decent job of finding bargain stocks, they have to increase returns by more than enough to offset their own salaries.

For these reasons, it is very difficult for even professional investors, such as mutual fund portfolio managers, to achieve a return greater than that shown by the market indexes. Therefore, we recommend that if you decide to invest in stocks, use index funds.

Myth 2: You Can Identify the Best Money Managers by Looking at Their Track Records

Occasionally you may be shown statistics ranking the performance of professionally managed funds. Beware of relying on such rankings, because they usually prove nothing. Testing for superior performance is a complicated statistical task, and the vast majority of performance studies are not done in a rigorous, unbiased fashion.

To see what is wrong with these studies, consider the following experiment. Imagine a coin-flipping contest with a million contestants. Each contestant flips a fair coin 10 times and the prize goes to the 1,000 contestants (0.1% of the one million) with the highest number of heads.

The possible outcomes for each contestant are from zero to 10 heads. Each contestant has exactly the same chance of winning because the outcome is entirely due to chance. We know with certainty that there will be 1,000 contestants who wind up as winners. Some may even have perfect track records: 10 heads. Nevertheless, it would not be valid to conclude that any of them has superior skill at flipping coins.

None of the winners would be entitled to boast that they are skilled coin flippers (although they might try to claim credit). The rankings are purely the result of chance, and skill plays no role. If the same one million contestants were to enter the same contest again, none of the previous winners would have a better chance of winning than the previous losers.

Picking stocks is not quite the same as flipping coins. **Even the most expert stock pickers will admit that chance plays a big role in explaining success in the stock market.** There is a saying often heard in the money management business: "It is better to be lucky than to be smart."

Therefore, studies of investment performance must be carefully designed to distinguish between skill and good luck. Scholars who have studied the performance of professionally managed funds have not found any convincing evidence that mutual funds that charge high fees deliver net returns that are higher than those delivered by passive index funds. Unless you have the ability to judge the statistical validity of the performance rankings you are looking at, you should not rely on them.

Myth 3: Stocks Are Not Risky in the Long Run

You explored this myth in some detail in Chapter 6, so we refer you to that chapter to review why this is a myth. As proven rigorously in the 1960s by Nobel-Prize winning economists Paul Samuelson and Robert C. Merton, there is no theoretical or historical reason to believe that stocks are *always* the best investment for investors with long-time horizons. On the contrary, there are groups of investors—stock brokers and entrepreneurs, for example—who by virtue of their professions probably are more exposed to stock market risk than they should be. If you are in a similar category, you should not invest heavily in stocks no matter how long your time horizon.

We are not recommending that everyone avoid stocks. There are very good reasons why some people should invest in stocks, and you may be one of those people. But do not invest in stocks on the grounds that your financial goal is 10 years in the future and because of that, stocks are the best way to achieve your goal.

Myth 4: Stocks Are the Best Hedge Against Inflation

There is no good evidence to support the proposition that stocks will protect you against inflation. In fact, there is considerable evidence to the contrary. The only time in the past century when there was persistent above-average inflation in the United States for a sustained period was the decade of the 1970s. The rate of inflation exceeded 3% in every year during that period. The Consumer Price Index (CPI) more than doubled, and the purchasing power of a dollar fell from $1 in January 1970 to 49 cents in December 1979. Just to keep pace with inflation, a dollar invested in the stock market would have had to more than double.

How did the U.S. stock market perform during the 1970s? Had you invested $10,000 in a portfolio of blue chip stocks on January 1, 1970, 10 years later, on December 31, 1979, your investment would have been worth $17,740. While stocks were returning 5.9% per year, inflation was eroding prices at a rate of 7.4% per year. That means it would have required $20,419 in December 1979 to buy what $10,000 would have bought in January 1970, but your investments grew to only $17,740. And that is after reinvesting all dividends! You lost a lot of purchasing power by being in stocks. Some inflation hedge!

Unfortunately, the government did not offer Treasury Inflation-Protected Securities (TIPS) in 1970, so your investment choices were limited, and ordinary government bonds did even worse than stocks. If you could have invested in inflation-protected bonds paying 3% per year in real interest (as you can today), your

$10,000 would have grown in purchasing power during those 10 years to $13,400. **The lesson is clear: The best inflation hedge is not stocks but inflation-protected bonds.**

Myth 5: Dollar Cost Averaging Improves Your Risk–Reward Tradeoff

Dollar cost averaging means investing a certain amount in stocks each month rather than investing the same total amount of money all at once. The proposition is that by doing so you improve your risk–reward tradeoff.

To try to show the superiority of a dollar-cost-averaging strategy, proponents often give examples showing that **when stock prices fluctuate, the average cost per share will always be less than the average price of a share.** This is indeed a mathematical fact.[1] **However, it does not follow that dollar cost averaging is a superior method of investing.**

For example, say you invest $1,000 every month for three months, instead of investing $3,000 all at once. Suppose the initial price of a share is $10 and that prices rise by $10 during each of the next two months, so that the sequence of monthly prices is:

$$\$10, \$20, \$30$$

The average price is $20.

---

1. It is, in particular, a mathematical instance known as "Jensen's Inequality."

Under dollar cost averaging, you will buy 100 shares in the first month, 50 shares in the second, and 33.3 shares in the third month. This is a total of 183.3 shares. Since you invested a total of $3,000, the average cost of a share will be $16.37. This is much less than the $20 average price.

But so what? Surely you would be better off to invest all $3,000 at the beginning of the three months. You would buy 300 shares at $10 per share and be much happier than if you had held back $2,000 in order to do dollar cost averaging.

Myth 6: An Age-Based Portfolio Strategy Is the Best Way to Secure Your Lifecycle Saving Targets

In recent years, investment companies have created so-called age-based portfolios intended for customers who are investing for retirement or for their children's college education. These funds typically offer a portfolio whose asset mix is predetermined to change year by year. The proportion invested in stocks starts out high and declines as the number of years left grows smaller.

A defining feature of these plans is that their asset mix does *not* depend on how the securities in the portfolio perform over time. Whether the stocks or bonds in the portfolio go up or down in value, the fractions invested in each asset class are readjusted each year according to a predetermined schedule.

If the intent is to guarantee that the retirement or college tuition target will be achieved or even made more likely, then such a strategy is not even approximately correct. Finance theory and practice have shown that a strategy designed to guarantee that a specific retirement or tuition target will be achieved must change the stock-bond mix *contingent on the performance of the portfolio* and not just on the passage of calendar time.

Age-based portfolios may serve to prevent inexperienced investors from making mistakes and taking unrecognized risks by investing in undiversified portfolios. However, as you saw in Chapters 3 and 4, the simplest way to be sure of reaching your retirement or college saving goal is to invest in I Bonds, TIPS, or other inflation-protected instruments.

In this chapter, you have considered some of the pitfalls of investing and how to avoid them. You also examined six major myths assumed in investing.

In the next chapter, you put it all together as you look more closely at the Six Steps to Worry-Free Investing we outlined in Chapter 1.

9

Putting It All Together

In this chapter you explore:

· Changing directions to a safer route

· Six Steps to Worry-Free Investing

· Tailoring a plan suited specifically to you

No matter where you are on your saving and investing journey, it is not too late to change direction, to pick a safer route to your destination. John Parker decided to adopt the new approach in his sixties to ensure that he and his wife, Joan, will have enough to live comfortably in retirement without fear that the stock market or inflation could rob them of their standard of living.

Paul Clark, who at 34 is far younger than John Parker, also has revisited his retirement saving plan and adopted a new approach, as you will see in this chapter. Both men have followed the Six Steps to Worry-Free Investing introduced back in Chapter 1:

1. **Set goals.**
2. **Specify targets.**
3. **Compute your required no-risk saving rate.**
4. **Determine your tolerance for risk.**
5. **Choose your risky asset portfolio.**
6. **Minimize taxes and transaction costs.**

Let's examine each of these steps in greater detail.

Step 1: Set Goals

Make a list of the specific goals you want to achieve through your saving and investment plan. You may have several goals, but the two most important are probably retirement and paying for a college education for your children.

If you are just starting your career, your salary may be much lower than you expect it to be later on. Medical doctors and other professionals often find themselves in this situation. Any saving you do may have to go toward paying off debts you incurred while getting your education. You may decide that it makes no sense for you to start saving for your children's college education or your own retirement until later in your career.

Chapter 9
Putting It All Together

Paul and Rita Clark live in Marysville, Ohio, and Paul has worked at the Honda plant since he was 21. Now that their two children, Mickey, 10, and Elisa, who is eight, are in school each day, Rita has picked up a job in marketing at the Scotts Lawn Company, where she specializes in sod and grass patches for golf courses. With their combined salaries they have not had trouble making the payments on their split-level ranch home, their two cars, both Hondas, and the family's usual outing each summer to Myrtle Beach.

Both Paul and Rita have retirement plans at their jobs. But talking with parents of college-age children at their jobs has caused them to realize what expenses might be involved. A college education is as important to a child as a high school education once was, but they had not made a conscious plan about how they might finance, or help finance, such advance schooling for Mickey and Elisa.

If you are a young couple like the Clarks, saving for your children's college education looms largest. Consider the strategic options that you have. You can, for example, opt to send the children to state schools. You can also require that the children, when they are old enough, save toward college by working in the summers. You may also ask them to work during college to help cover the costs. Perhaps your children are smart enough to be candidates for academic scholarships, or athletes talented enough to get athletic scholarships.

Unfortunately, the Clarks don't think they can rely on their children getting such scholarships. They think it is better to assume they will have to carry the whole burden and then be pleasantly surprised if it turns out that they don't.

Most people postpone serious planning for retirement until they are 35 or 40 years of age. At around 50 or 55, you might be seriously thinking more specifically about what living standard you want when you retire. Like the Parkers, you will have to address some important lifestyle issues.

Will you stay in the same area, or will you move to an area with a lower cost of living? Do you want the same size house, or will you want a smaller, more economical one with lower taxes? Do you expect your retirement home to cost less than what you can sell your current home for? If so, you may be able to roll the profit into your retirement account. Or do you instead want a house or condominium on a golf course somewhere that may be as expensive, or even more expensive, as your current home?

The chief advantage the Clarks have is that they are still young enough to take steps now that can matter by the time their children are college age. Rita searched the Internet for college savings plans, and Paul spoke to a financial counselor in his Human Resources department who called a friend at Ohio State. They both began to hear more about 529 plans, and though they were just beginning their search they were on the right path toward the most worry-free means of reaching college education goals for both children. Knowing their goal was the important first step.

Step 2: Specify Targets

The College Goal

If you are saving and investing for a child's college education you should visit *www.collegeispossible.org* and *www.collegeboard.com* to learn the costs associated with the specific schools you would like your child to attend. If you find you are considering schools where the tuition, room, and board average $22,000 a year, you know you have to save $88,000 in today's dollars. If your child is three years old, you have 15 years before the first payment is due to the college of choice and 19 years before the last payment is due.

For the 2001–2002 college year, the College Board estimated total expenses could range from $10,367 for an out-of-state student at a two-year public institution to $17,740 for an out-of-state student at a four-year public university, to $26,093 for a four-year private university. Remember, these are average costs across the nation. Actual costs may be higher or lower, depending on the region. Costs are highest in the New England area, probably because of the Ivy League schools, and lowest in the Southwest.

The average total cost for private four-year colleges in New England was $32,326, and that was significantly below what Bill and Mary Sullivan, whom you met back in Chapter 4, faced when their daughter, Ruthie, was accepted at Stanford. Because of the bear market, Ruthie would not be attending Stanford unless she got aid. Even Penn State would be a stretch. Bob and Sandy Adams faced similar downsizing of their dreams for son Chuck's education. Paul and Rita Clark, fortunately, realized their goal early enough to do something constructive, and part of that meant cutting down on some expenses and getting enough money invested in the right plan, one that could minimize the impact of inflation.

College expenses have been rising far faster than inflation. According to the Bureau of Labor Statistics, college cost inflation has exceeded the general rate of inflation in the Consumer Price Index (CPI) at an average of 4.33% per year since 1981. The share of family income required to pay total college expenses increased for many families during the 1980s and 1990s, but it went up most for those with low to moderate income.

These figures are troubling because they mean that even for your child to attend a local four-year public college or university, you must save at least enough to generate approximately $12,000 a year for four years—in today's dollars—and you must invest that money in such a way that it will be safe and its investment return will at least keep pace with the rate of increase of college costs. If you wish your child to attend a private four-year college, your savings will need to generate at least $26,000 a year, in today's terms, more if you are looking at the Northeast. As most parents of college students discover, there are always expenses not figured into the official college expenses, such as fraternity or sorority dues, the costs of bringing the student home during the holidays, and spending money.

To be conservative you should start saving for a child's education soon after he or she is born, perhaps using gifts provided by grandparents. Take advantage of the special tax incentives designed to encourage college saving. Set up a Section 529 account, and select state plans that provide low-risk investment options like prepaid tuition and CollegeSure® Certificates of Deposits (CDs). Visit *www.529.com* for a complete listing of the various state plans available. Consider buying I Bonds through payroll deduction as a means of automatically investing part of each paycheck for a child's education. When I Bonds are redeemed to pay for college expenses, they qualify for tax exemption (subject to certain income limits).

Beware of college investment programs that provide age-based portfolios of stocks and bonds. Age-based investment strategies are based on the logically flawed notion that the risk of stocks diminishes over time. Unless they offer guarantees, these plans generally expose you to significant risk of falling short of your target.

You should revisit your target each year. If you were planning on sending your child to a public college or university, you may find your child is a talented enough student to get into a top private school. You would have to raise your saving target. Or, vice versa, you may have been aiming for a top private school and find your child is not a motivated student. You may want to lower your sights to a less-expensive public college.

The Retirement Goal

If you are saving for retirement, we recommend starting by figuring out how much you would need to maintain your *minimum acceptable* lifestyle. We recommend that you aim at achieving the *minimum acceptable* target **with certainty**. You do not want to undershoot this target. If you feel that you can save more than this minimum, the additional savings can be invested in the stock market to take a chance at earning potentially higher returns.

Retirement experts calculate you will need at least 70% of your preretirement income to maintain your preretirement standard of living once you retire. John and Joan Parker had been aiming at just over 70% of John's income of $135,000 a year. After the market plunge, they would have fallen far short of that if they had continued with their plans to retire at 62.

The experts estimate you will need less to live on in retirement than you need while you are working because many of your day-to-day expenses are connected with earning a living. For example, after you retire you will not have commuting costs, whether by car or by public transportation. Even if you continue to maintain two cars in the family, the number of miles put on them will most likely drop substantially, with resulting savings in fuel and maintenance costs unless you plan a heavy travel schedule.

In addition, the current amount you spend on work clothes will virtually disappear. Buying lunches at work is far more expensive than having lunch at home. In addition, you will not be saving for retirement. The savings component of income will be available for you to live on now.

For these and other reasons your living costs should drop once you retire. If you are earning $50,000 a year now, you will need to generate the equivalent of $35,000 a year in retirement ($50,000 x 0.7) to pay for your *minimum acceptable* living standard in retirement, assuming your salary keeps pace with inflation. If you are earning $100,000 a year, you will need to generate an inflation-adjusted $70,000 a year to maintain your current living standard.

Step 3: Compute Your Required No-Risk Saving Rate

Now, using the Worry-Free Investing (WFI) calculator we have supplied on our Web site (*www.prenhall.com/worryfree/*), calculate the amount of money you must have in your retirement saving accounts (your 401(k) or 403(b) plan, your IRAs, etc.) the day you retire to be certain you can afford that *minimum acceptable* living standard. The older you are, and the less you have already saved, the larger the annual savings figure will be. But remember to take into account the amount you will receive from Social Security. It can significantly reduce the amounts you need to save in your other retirement savings plans.

You may also be covered by an old-fashioned defined benefit pension plan. A defined benefit plan promises you a fixed annual income for as long as you and your spouse live, usually based on how long you work for your employer and on your salary in your final years of employment. If you have some coverage from a defined benefit plan, it, too, should be subtracted from the amount you need to save each year in your 401(k) plan or IRA.

But, beware, because very few defined benefit plans in the United States index their benefits for inflation. Most companies adjust the benefit for inflation only at irregular intervals, and not very generously. If allowed (and some companies do allow this), you would be better off taking any benefit from a defined benefit pension plan as a lump sum when you retire and investing that amount in an inflation-protected life annuity like the Inflation Proofer or a portfolio of Treasury Inflation-Protected Securities (TIPS).

You can still find an Inflation Proofer quote at *client.annuitynetadvisor.com/decisions/annuity_quote.asp*, but be warned that the annuity itself is not currently for sale. Figure out how large an annuity your lump sum pension benefit will be, and then treat it as an addition to your expected Social Security income in retirement.

Step 4: Determine Your Tolerance for Risk

Unless you save more than the amount necessary to achieve your minimum acceptable standard of living at retirement, you will have no need for this step and the next. This step is for you to decide how much risk to take in the risky part of your investment portfolio. Having secured the most important of your goals, you may be willing to take considerable risk with your extra savings.

In Chapter 7, you saw how you might be able to gain some exposure to the potentially higher returns of the stock market without taking significant risk by using long-term options to supplement the returns of the TIPS. This strategy is an excellent one once you are retired and free of the restraints employers place on 401(k) investments.

However, such long-term options may not be usable while you are still accumulating your retirement savings. Most employers prohibit the use of options in 401(k) and similar plans. Only if you had significant savings outside the 401(k) plan would you be able to use the long-term options strategy. You could use those savings to buy the options in an effort to earn equity-like returns to enhance the TIPS returns.

Step 5: Choose Your Risky Asset Portfolio

If the bulk of your retirement savings is in your 401(k) plan, you may be at risk. You examined a model in Chapter 7 for calculating whether or not it might be appropriate for you to take some risk by investing in stocks. You should use this model to determine if it is appropriate for you, given your situation, to take any stock risk.

If you decide to take some risk, you must consider the consequences if your stock investments should under-perform. Would you be willing to work a few years more to make up the losses? Would you be able to increase your savings rate to make up for any losses? You should only take risk in your retirement investments as long as any losses won't seriously damage your retirement income or plans, or you are young and have a stable job with bright prospects for advancement, and hence greater income in the future that will make additional saving easier.

Step 6: Minimize Taxes and Transaction Costs

Taxes, and the costs of managing your investments, which are known as *transactions costs,* can greatly reduce your retirement savings. The government, in an effort to encourage you to save for retirement and for college, has provided a number of ways to invest that are free of taxes. You can avoid taxes by establishing a 529 plan for college, 401(k), 403(b), or similar employer-sponsored retirement plans, or Individual Retirement Accounts (IRAs). TIPS are best held in such plans. Otherwise, you must pay taxes every year on the interest earned. Inside the 401(k) plan, 403(b) plan, or IRA, the interest earned is not taxed. I Bonds, on the other hand, are tax deferred even when held outside of a 529 or retirement account.

I Bonds have no fees or other charges. You can buy them at your local bank or online at *www.savingsbonds.gov/sav/sbiinvst.htm.* You can avoid most fees on buying or selling TIPS and other U.S. Treasury securities by using TreasuryDirect. TreasuryDirect charges a very small annual account maintenance fee—currently $25—and allows you to call the shots from the privacy and comfort of home. Its Web site is at *www.savingsbonds.gov/sec/ secinvsr.htm* or call 800-722-2678.

If you invest in stocks, minimize your taxes and transaction costs by using index funds. By doing so, you will increase your chances of earning the returns you hope to achieve.

In this chapter, you have explored in greater depth the Six Steps to Worry-Free Investing. You now have everything you need to tailor a plan suitable to your individual needs. Does this mean you are no longer ever going to need the advice of a professional advisor? That's up to you. If you still find the terms and detail of investing to be uncomfortably complex, you may want advice. The next chapter considers whether or not you might need an advisor.

C H A P T E R

10

Do You Need Professional Advice?

In this chapter, you explore:

· Whether or not you need a financial advisor

· Fee advisors versus commission advisors

· How to evaluate advisors

M ary Elliott Kelsey from Milwaukee, Wisconsin, is an informed investor. She reads *The Wall Street Journal* each day and subscribes to a multitude of online investment newsletters. She discusses trends with friends at her health club, and she watches CNBC. Yet, it seems, the more she absorbs, the harder it is to fully understand it all.

"It's like the weather," she told her best friend, Gladys. "The more the weather person knows about pressure fronts, Doppler reports, midlatitudinal cyclone belts, and all that, the harder it must be to know about what weather we really are going to have. Everything's in percentages now. Sixty percent chance of rain. Even then, it's still just an educated guess, for which I think those weather people are wrong as often as they are right. I feel like that when I try to figure out what's really going on with trends in the financial world."

In this book, we have tried to share clear steps you can take toward lowered risk investing. Many of the avenues you have explored weren't even around a few years ago, and others will inevitably change in the future. How can you possibly keep up?

Mary Elliott Kelsey's needs are complex. When she married Raymond Kelsey, he was a librarian in the city's public library. He liked books but not those with numbers in them, so he passed along the checkbook and all other financial matters to Mary. She liked keeping them on budget and headed toward the future, which included the futures of their two children, Trent and Michael, who are both still in school. Mary is 36, Raymond is 42, and her constant vigilance has resulted in financial goals that include:

- A risk-free retirement fund for herself and Raymond that would allow their dream of traveling one day
- College funds for both boys at whatever schools they wish to attend

· Purchase of a house in a way that will let them maximize the
equity when it comes time to retire

Mary has embraced all the ideas found in this book and feels confident she can manage their two incomes to meet their established goals. Nevertheless, even though she's scoured the Internet
and exhausted her own knowledge and that of her friends, she
still has questions. Investment, with its constantly changing laws
and regulations, as well as ups and downs, remains a labyrinth
even to someone as well informed as she is. She wishes she could
sit down and pick the brain of a professional who would be interested in clarifying and supporting her goals, instead of shifting
her to investment programs that merely generate better commissions for the advisor. Is this too much to ask?

**To have an advisor or not to have an advisor? That is
the question. It's a good one. In a way, this book
seeks to advise you. But we address only the investment part of financial planning. You may need help
with other key parts of developing a long-term financial plan.**

So who needs an advisor? Certainly anyone who does not feel
confident he or she can apply the lessons of this book. Even if you
agree with the ideas in this book, you may need help actually
pulling the trigger to make the changes necessary to apply this
new approach. If you have difficulty picking up the phone to sell
your current mutual funds to buy Treasury Inflation-Protected
Securities (TIPS), we suggest you need a financial planner or an

investment advisor. You may not feel comfortable buying I Bonds or TIPS from TreasuryDirect or getting online to buy an inflation-indexed annuity. A financial advisor can help.

Your needs may be more fundamental than that. You may need help setting up a budget and sticking to it so you can achieve your goals. Consider hiring a financial planner. You may need help with setting up wills or trusts to protect your assets for your children. Get it. You may need guidance as to how much insurance and what kinds of insurance you need, other than basic house and life insurance. Seek help. You may forget to revisit your plan on a regular basis to make sure you are still on target.

In many cases, the laws in your state may vary enough that you need professional advice about them. You can search the Internet, but how do you interpret the vast flow of information available? You may very well need to speak to someone with professional understanding. We encourage you to do so.

Many Kinds of Advisors

You can choose from many kinds of financial advisors. There are professionals called financial planners or financial advisors. Others call themselves investment advisors. Almost anyone can call himself or herself a "financial advisor" in most states, but true financial planners and advisors have training in a broad array of financial and investment matters. A number of colleges around the country offer degrees in financial planning. These provide the most rigorous training in financial planning available and address all the important aspects of financial planning, not simply investments.

Many more financial planners have passed a less rigorous, but still quite challenging, financial planning course at the College for Financial Planning, and as a result, can attach the designation CFP to their names. This means they are Certified Financial Planners. They have taken courses not only in investing, but also in insurance, tax law, pension law, and trust law, though in most states they are not licensed to sell insurance until they take additional courses and pass additional tests. Likewise, they are not lawyers, though they know enough to advise you when you need the help of a lawyer. They are required to take additional hours of training each year to maintain their accreditation.

Some accountants and lawyers will provide financial planning and investment advice. Certified Public Accountants (CPAs) who specialize in financial planning will often have the designation Personal Financial Specialist (PFS) after their names. Insurance agents who have passed courses in financial planning will have Chartered Financial Counselor (ChFC) after their names. Others call themselves investment advisors and will often have the Certified Investment Advisor (CIMA), Certified Investment Management Consultant (CIMC), or Registered Investment Adviser (RIA) after their names. Often these people will have investment training but will not have taken more complete financial planning training. Be aware that some of those offering you financial planning advice have been trained primarily to sell you insurance, stocks, bonds, or mutual funds.

Assuming you want a true financial planner, the first cut in choosing one should be to seek out one with appropriate training. That means choosing one with at least a bachelor's degree in a financial planning major, or with a CFP, CPA-PFS, or ChFC designation. You can often find such people in the yellow pages of your local phone book, but the Financial Planning Association in Atlanta and Denver also has a directory of its members by region, so you can find candidates in your area. This can be accessed through its Web site *www.fpanet.org*. The American Institute of Certified Public Accountants also lists accountants with financial planning practices on its Web site: *www.aicpa.org/members/div/pfp/index*.

You may feel you only need help implementing your college or retirement investment advice. In that case, someone with a CIMA or CIMC designation may be sufficient.

How to Find an Advisor You Can Trust

An important aspect of any relationship is trust. When that relationship is with someone who handles all the important money you own, this is even more so. Before selecting an advisor, you should interview several. You must be comfortable with the person you hire. You must be satisfied with his or her expertise. You must be confident he or she will give you unbiased advice, and then carry out your instructions. You should ask each candidate for references, and then check them.

Here are some important things to keep in mind.

First, check the credentials. What training does the candidate advisor have? Does he or she have a degree in financial planning? Ask to see it. If not, is he or she a CFP/CPA-PFS or ChFC? Ask to see the appropriate credentials. Even if you just want an investment advisor, ask to see the CIMC, CIMA, or RIA credentials.

Second, how is the advisor compensated? **Some advisors earn their income through commissions generated when they buy mutual funds or buy or sell shares for you.** That should not automatically disqualify them, but it is a warning flag. Some advisors have been known to recommend the buying and selling of stocks or funds for clients simply to generate more commission income for themselves. Such an advisor may not be interested in taking you as a client when you explain you want all or most of your investments in TIPS or I Bonds because there is little or no commission from such investments. Even an honest commission-based advisor may not accept you as a client for this reason.

Many advisors charge a fee rather than relying on commissions. The fee may be a percentage of the assets in your financial plan, or it may be a flat fee per year, or it may be an hourly rate like that charged by lawyers and accountants. A fee-based advisor offering the full range of financial planning advice may charge you a higher fee than one offering only investment help. Since you may want help primarily in executing a plan you have already decided on using TIPS, inflation-protected annuities, I Bonds, and perhaps a small amount of stocks, you may be able to negotiate a lower fee than the advisor normally charges. After all, you will not be taking as much of his or her time as a regular client. Although many commission-based advisors give good advice, we believe you are more likely to get unbiased help and advice in this case from a fee-based advisor.

Again, check those references. Are they happy with the guidance they have received from the planner? Does the planner listen to what is required? Does he or she regularly review the plan with the client to see that needs have not changed and that the plan is still on target? Is the reference still using the planner? If not, why not?

Here are a few questions to consider when seeking an advisor:

- Does the advisor know the difference among, for example, TIPS, I Bonds, and Long-Term Equity Anticipation Securities (LEAPS)? If you get a head scratch and puzzled look, it's best to keep shopping.

- Has a friend, relative, or colleague had a positive and trustworthy experience with the advisor?

- Did the advisor ever make money when clients lost theirs?

- Does the advisor realistically consider your wishes and needs first?

- Does the advisor work for a company that the advisor is obliged to favor?

The last one on the list can be a real problem as you implement your plan because the advisor may be obliged to try to persuade you of the merits of a different plan so he or she can sell you his or her company's products. If the advisor makes such an attempt, don't hire him or her.

If there is a Better Business Bureau in your area, check with them once you have cut the number of candidates to a small number. Ask if any complaints have been lodged against any of your candidates, and ask for the outcome.

Now that you have read this book, you may want to follow its steps but feel you need help to tailor them to the needs of your own worry-free investment plan. Then you should seek an advisor. Make sure it is someone who agrees with your strategy and is willing to help you execute your plan, buying the securities and discussing specific laws and conditions that may apply to your case. This applies in particular to 529 college savings plans, since every state has variations, its own applications, or no such available option at all.

We hope advisors will encourage their clients to read this book and then help them follow its path. What any advisor brings to the table is experience buying and selling securities, comfort in actually carrying out any decision to buy or sell, and a more thorough understanding of investing and of the laws and conditions specific to your state and area. He or she can help you put your plan into place by helping you sell any investments you already have that don't fit the new plan. He or she can, in effect, hold your hand and encourage you while you make the change.

In this chapter, you considered the fact that many avenues explored in this book weren't around a few years ago and that other changes will inevitably occur in the future. How can you possibly keep up?

You understand the importance of keeping current and that hiring a financial advisor may be very beneficial to you. You also looked at how you can choose the right financial planner.

In many cases, the laws in your state vary enough that you need professional advice about them. You can search the Internet on your own, but you may need an advisor to help you interpret the vast flow of information available.

In addition, we hope that advisors will encourage their clients to read this book and then help them follow its path.

You have, at this point, completed all you need to know about beginning to assemble your own worry-free investment strategy.

Good investing!

In the following chapters, we provide greater depth for those who wish to dig a bit deeper into topics covered earlier for a better understanding of our plan. In addition, we provide some good resources to help you implement your new financial plan.

2

Further Food for Thought

11

Real-Life Examples of Worry-Free Retirement Investing

In this chapter, you explore:

· How to apply the Six Steps to Worry-Free Investing

· How to calculate needs in various circumstances

· How to combine Treasury Inflation-Protected Securities (TIPS) and I Bonds with 401(k)s and Individual Retirement Accounts (IRAs)

Paul Younger

Paul Younger has a good life. He is 30 years old, has a degree from the University of Wisconsin, and works as a technician at a television station. He earns $30,000 a year and is unmarried, though his girlfriend, who has a small child, lives with him. He's not living high, but he's comfortable in Madison, Wisconsin, enjoys sailing on Lake Mendota on the weekends and taking in shows and concerts when they come to town. He is buying a small Cape Cod-style house in Shorewood

Hills, a suburb, and is paying off a second-hand Jeep Cherokee in addition to his small sailboat. He has insured all of these against disaster. Except for the hours he works—he starts each day before dawn—life is good.

At 30, he is a long way from retirement, yet he has thought about it a little, and he participates in the company's 401(k) retirement savings plan. In fact, he contributes 6% of his salary to the plan, and the company matches the contribution 50 cents for each dollar he contributes. "I'd like to contribute more," he says, "but it's tough with the house, SUV, and boat payments on top of daily living costs." If he could afford to do so, Paul could legally contribute up to 15% of his salary ($4,500) a year pretax to the 401(k) plan, but the company matches only until its contribution equals 3% of his pay.

Paul is like many other young people today who are already saving for retirement, thanks to their companies' 401(k) plans. They have accepted the reality that they will have to provide most of their own retirement income. Relatively few workers today are covered by the old company-sponsored defined benefit plans that paid a monthly pension until death. Many young workers also suspect that Social Security benefits will be cut substantially before they are old enough to collect. Many are coming to realize they have to start saving for retirement early and that investing for retirement is a lifelong process.

Paul is contributing $1,800 each year (6% of his salary) to the company 401(k) plan, reducing his taxable income by that amount. His company contributes an additional $900 per year

(3% of his salary), so Paul's account grew by $2,700 last year. He has been in the plan for five years and has $9,664 in his account. His aggressive asset allocation has hurt him in the past two years. At present, Paul has 30% of his 401(k) assets invested in a stock index fund, 20% in a large cap growth fund, 20% in a small cap growth fund, 20% in a small cap value fund, and 10% in a foreign stock fund. Recently a new option was announced, a Treasury Inflation-Protected Securities (TIPS) fund that invests in U.S. Treasury inflation-protected bonds of all maturities.

Let's see how Paul Younger would apply the Six Steps to Worry-Free Investing:

Step 1: Set Goals

Paul's goal is retirement. He plans to retire at 67, the age that people in his age group can receive full Social Security retirement benefits.

Step 2: Specify Targets

Paul assumes he will need 70% of his current income, $21,000 in today's dollars, to maintain his current lifestyle when he retires.

Step 3: Compute Your Required No-Risk Saving Rate

As you saw in Chapter 3, the method for computing Paul's required saving rate consists of several steps:

a. First, get an estimate of Paul's expected Social Security benefit at age 67. Using the Quick Calculator at the Social Security Administration's Web site, *www.ssa.gov/OACT/ quickcalc/calculator.html*, we find that his expected monthly benefit is $1,151, which is $13,812 per year.

b. Subtract this from Paul's target income of $21,000 to get $7,188 as the annual amount that must come from his retirement saving.

c. To compute how much Paul needs in his retirement account at age 67 to be able to withdraw $7,188 per year for the rest of his life, we have two choices. We can either estimate Paul's life expectancy (using a calculator such as the one at *www.northwesternmutual.com/corporate/newsmedia/ longevitygame.html*) and compute the amount he will need by using the formula in Chapter 3, or we can look up the cost of a lifetime inflation-proof annuity of $7,188 per year at Annuitynet.com. Using the first approach, let's assume that Paul's life expectancy is 87 years. That means he needs enough for 20 years in retirement. From Chapter 3, the formula for the present value is:

$$PV = \frac{1 - \dfrac{1}{(1+i)^n}}{i} X$$

Substituting into this formula .03 for the real rate of interest or i, 20 years for n, and $7,188 for X, the sum he needs at age 67 is $106,939. You can also do this calculation using the online Worry-Free Investing (WFI) calculator at our Web site (*www.prenhall.com/worryfree/*):

WFI Calculations for Amount Needed

Amount Needed at Retirement	
Number of years	20
Interest rate	3%
Target retirement income	$7,188
Amount required at retirement	**$106,939**

According to AnnuityNet.com (*client.annuitynetadvisor.com/ decisions/annuity_quote.asp*), the quoted price for an inflation-proof life annuity of $600 per month is $107,500, which is pretty close to $106,939. Let's use the higher number, $107,500.

d. The next step is to calculate how much of Paul's salary to save each year to reach that goal. He has 37 years until he retires. He has already saved $9,664 in his 401(k) account. The future value of this amount at retirement is given by the formula:

$$FV = PV(1+i)^n$$

Substituting $9,664 for *PV*, .03 for *i*, and 37 for *n*, we find that *FV* = $28,849. So we subtract this from the $107,500 needed at retirement, and that leaves $78,650.

To find the annual contribution needed to reach that target, we can use the formula you learned in Chapter 3:[1]

$$FV = \frac{(1+i)^{n+1} - (1+i)}{i} X$$

FV stands for future value, i for the interest rate, n for the number of years, and X for the annual contribution. In this case, FV is $78,650, i is .03, and n is 37. Substituting them into the formula, we find that the annual contribution X is $1,154.[2]

Thus, in order to be able to take out a retirement benefit of $7,188 per year for 20 years, Paul would need to save $1,154 per year for the next 37 years. This is 3.85% of his $30,000 salary.

Paul is currently contributing 6% of his salary ($1,800) to his 401(k) plan, and his employer is contributing another 3% ($900), for a total of 9% ($2,700). In other words, he is saving 5.15% more of his salary than he needs to achieve a 70% replacement rate. This leaves him a comfortable margin

---

1. This is the formula for the future value of an *immediate annuity*. This means contributions start immediately, at the *beginning* of the year.
2. Using the online WFI calculator at our Web site to do this, you find:
   WFI Calculations for Annual Contributions Required
   Number of Years: 37
   Interest rate: 3%
   Target future value: $78,650
   Annual contribution required: $1,154

of safety in case Social Security benefits are cut or the real interest rate is less than the assumed 3% rate per year.

Step 4: Determine Your Tolerance for Risk

Since Paul is still young, the greatest part of his earning power lies ahead of him. His job at the television station is in the state capital, which has shown significant ability to resist economic downturns, so there is only moderate job risk. Paul has been taking business management courses at a local college to improve his job prospects if he should decide to leave the television industry.

Besides his 401(k) balance, his assets include his equity in his house, which he bought three years ago, his SUV, and his boat. The house is an asset that should grow in value in line with his principal repayments and inflation.

All in all, Paul's circumstances indicate a fairly high tolerance for risk.

Step 5: Choose Your Risky Asset Portfolio

Paul's current 401(k) asset allocation is quite risky. It is all invested in stocks. He has 30% of his 401(k) assets invested in a stock index fund, 20% in a large cap growth fund, 20% in a small cap growth fund, 20% in a small cap value fund, and 10% in a foreign stock fund. Since his employer is now offering a TIPS fund as a new alternative asset class, Paul could play it safe with part of his retirement money and leave the rest in equities.

For example, suppose that he transfers the $9,664 he now has into the TIPS fund and invests his employer's future matching contributions (3% of his salary) in the TIPS fund. This would provide a secure income to supplement his Social Security income starting at age 67. If he invests his own continuing 401(k) contributions (6% of his salary) in the current mix of equity funds he has chosen, he might get lucky and be able to retire early. If the stocks do badly, his desired minimum living standard is still safe.

Step 6: Minimize Taxes and Transaction Costs

By saving through his 401(k) plan, Paul is avoiding the payment of income taxes on his investment earnings until he withdraws income in retirement. This is about the best he or anyone can do.

He should check the management fees he is being charged on the equity funds he has chosen in his 401(k) plan. The stock index fund probably has the lowest fees. It is doubtful that higher fees on the other equity funds are justified in terms of better performance. Index funds have historically outperformed most actively managed funds. He would almost surely be better off transferring all the money in the equity funds to the index fund.

You, like Paul Younger, may feel you are well positioned for retirement if you have a 401(k) or similar plan and are contributing regularly to it. You may think that with the amount you are contributing, the amount your employer is contributing, and given the historic returns on stocks, you should be in good shape to retire. You may feel you don't have to save outside the retirement plan. That's not necessarily so. Take a look at another example.

Mary and Marty Mature

Mary and Marty Mature are both 45 years old, married with two children, and they intend to retire at age 67. Mary earns $50,000 a year as a middle manager for an insurance company in Raleigh, North Carolina. She has just begun contributing to her company's 401(k) plan because she joined the insurance company only a year ago, moving from a smaller company that had no plan. She contributes 6% of pay, and the company matches her contribution to the plan 50 cents for each dollar she contributes (just as Paul's employer did in our previous example). These are close to national averages for employer and employee contributions.

Mary contributed $2,000 to an Individual Retirement Account (IRA) most years while working for several smaller companies and has about $53,000 in it. It is 100% invested in stocks. She has not contributed to the IRA since joining the 401(k) plan, though she still is eligible to do so.

Mary's husband, Marty, is also 45 years old. He works as a repairman for a real estate management company and earns $25,000 a year. His employer has no retirement plan, though Marty has contributed to his own IRA for the past seven years and has a little more than $13,000 in it. It, too, is invested 100% in stocks.

The Matures own a modest home in a middle class suburb, and since they closed on it 15 years ago, the mortgage payments are easily manageable. Furthermore, the value of their house has more than doubled.

Mary and Marty live comfortably. They eat out at a local restaurant almost every week and play golf at a local public golf course most weekends. They vacation for a week at Myrtle Beach or on the Outer Banks each summer, renting a condominium.

But the question is: Will Mary and Marty have enough for a comfortable retirement?

Let's see how they would apply the Six Steps to Worry-Free Investing:

Step 1: Set Goals

Marty and Mary's goal is retirement. They plan to retire in 22 years at age 67.

Step 2: Specify Targets

Their combined income is $75,000. They assume they will need 70% of that, $52,500 per year in today's dollars, to maintain their current lifestyle when they retire.

Step 3: Compute Your Required No-Risk Saving Rate

As you saw in Chapter 3, the method for computing the Matures' required saving rate consists of several steps:

a. First, get an estimate of their expected Social Security benefits at age 67. Using the Quick Calculator at the Social Security Administration's Web site, *www.ssa.gov/OACT/quickcalc/ calculator.html,* we find that Mary's expected monthly benefit is $1,551.00, which is $18,612 per year. Marty's is $968 per month, which is $11,616. The combined total is $30,228.

b. Subtract this from their target income of $52,500 to get $22,272 as the annual amount that must come from retirement saving.

c. To find out how much they need in their retirement account at age 67, we will assume a combined life expectancy of 95 years. That means they need enough for 28 years in retirement. From Chapter 3, the formula for the present value of an annual amount is:

$$PV = \frac{1 - \dfrac{1}{(1+i)^n}}{i} X$$

Assuming a 3% real rate of interest or i, n is 28 years, and X is $22,272, we find the sum they need at age 67 to be about $417,914.

If we use the AnnuityNet.com calculator, the quoted price for an inflation-proof joint life annuity of $22,272 per year ($1,856 per month) is $425,000. We will use this number.

The next step is to calculate how much of their salary they need to save each year to reach that goal. They have 22 years until they plan to retire. Mary already has $53,000 in her IRA,

and Marty has $13,000 in his, for a combined total of
$66,000. Again, we are assuming they will earn a real interest
rate of 3% per year. The formula for computing the amount
this will grow to by retirement is:

$$FV = PV(1+i)^n$$

Substituting $66,000 for PV, .03 for i, and 22 for n, we find
that FV = $126,463. So we subtract this from the $425,000
needed at retirement, and that leaves $298,537.

Now we use the formula to find the annual contribution
needed to reach a desired future value:[3]

$$FV = \frac{(1+i)^{n+1} - (1+i)}{i} X$$

In this case, FV is $298,537, i is .03, and n is 22. Substituting
these values into the formula, we find that the annual
contribution X is $9,492. This is 12.66% of their $75,000 per
year in combined salaries. They will have to tighten their belts
and take advantage of every possible tax-advantaged
retirement saving option. This means Mary will have to
contribute the maximum she is allowed under her employer's
401(k) plan, and Marty will contribute as much as he can to
his IRA.

---

3. This is the formula for the future value of an *immediate annuity*. This means contributions start immediately, at the *beginning* of the year.

Step 4: Determine Your Tolerance for Risk

Both Mary and Marty's job risk is relatively low, but **they are well along in their working careers. They will not be able to offset as much stock market risk with their future earning power as a younger couple could.** For them, a key consideration in deciding how much to invest in stocks is their willingness to postpone their retirement should their portfolio not perform well.

They are very reluctant to postpone retirement past age 67, so they decide to invest as much of their retirement saving as they can in inflation-protected bonds. Since they are free to choose where they invest the money in their IRAs, they decide to move it all to a mutual fund company that offers a TIPS fund.

Unfortunately, Mary's new employer does not offer a TIPS fund as one of the choices in the company's 401(k) plan. Mary has a choice of several mutual funds, including a stock index fund. The safest 401(k) alternative available to her is a stable value fund offering a rate of interest that varies from year to year.

Step 5: Choose Your Risky Asset Portfolio

Mary decides to allocate all her 401(k) money to the stable value fund. In part, this is because she wants to avoid risk, but in part, it is motivated by her desire to shield the investment income from taxes.

Step 6: Minimize Taxes and Transaction Costs

Mary and Marty will shelter most of their retirement investments from taxes by keeping them in their IRAs and in Mary's new 401(k) account at work. If Mary and Marty decide to invest some of their money in stocks, they will do that with the savings that they hold outside of their tax-sheltered retirement accounts. Because much of the return they expect to receive on stocks will come in the form of an increase in price, they can defer paying taxes until they sell the stocks. Interest earnings held outside of their retirement accounts, on the other hand, will be taxed immediately.

One way for them to shelter at least part of their additional savings is to put more into their IRAs. Since, in this example, Mary's earnings are less than $60,000 per year in 2001 (you should visit the IRS Web site and check Publication 590 to see what the current year's income figure is since it changes from year to year), she can still contribute up to $2,000 a year pretax to an IRA, even though her employer offers a retirement plan. If she earned more than $60,000 a year, because her employer offers a retirement plan, she could not contribute to a regular IRA, though she might be able to contribute to a Roth IRA.

Since she has previously invested through a regular IRA, Mary knows it allows her to deduct her contribution from her income before computing income taxes. The IRA contribution reduces her taxable income and the amount of taxes she owes. The government is encouraging her (and you) to save for retirement by not taxing until retirement any income saved in an IRA.

Mary will pay no income taxes on the investment returns of the investments in the IRA until she starts to take them out after retirement, so they grow much more quickly than in an account where she would pay taxes on the investment returns each year. When Mary retires, her income taxes should be lower because her income will be lower. However, if Mary should take any money out of the IRA before she retires, she would owe ordinary income tax and a penalty tax on that money.

Within the IRA, Mary can use the full range of investments— stocks, bonds, stock and bond mutual funds, money market funds, etc. We recommend Mary instead invest heavily in TIPS within her IRA. Remember, with TIPS you receive your investment return twice a year, and outside an IRA Mary would have to pay income taxes on that investment return. Inside an IRA, however, the investment return will be exempt from taxes until she begins withdrawing it at retirement.

Of course, Mary could invest in stocks in the hopes of achieving a higher return and take the chance of losing all or some of her investment. But this is serious money, something that must be there when she retires. As John and Joan Parker discovered back in Chapter 1, stock returns are unreliable. Instead, we suggest Mary put all of her IRA savings into TIPS. Mary can buy TIPS directly from the Treasury using its TreasuryDirect program. She can get more information from the Treasury's Web site: *www.treasurydirect.gov*. The only restriction is that TIPS must be bought in minimum amounts of $1,000.

Since Marty is not covered by an employer pension plan, he can boost his IRA savings from $2,000 a year to $3,000 a year. His IRA has also been invested in stocks just like Mary's. Our advice would be the same for Marty as it was for Mary—invest his IRA in TIPS.

After making their maximum allowable contributions to Mary's 401(k) and their IRAs, Mary and Marty may decide they do not want to take any risk with their additional savings. In that case, we recommend I Bonds. With I Bonds, the federal government will not tax the investment return until they sell the bonds. Since Marty and Mary are buying the bonds for their retirement, sale most likely will be at retirement when their income tax rate should be lower. State and local governments do not tax the investment return of I Bonds at any time. As noted, I Bonds, like TIPS, pay a real return guaranteed by the federal government over and above inflation. The returns from stocks and ordinary bonds are not guaranteed, and so may be eroded by inflation.

It will not be easy for Mary and Marty. They will have to cut back on some of their spending. They may be able to play golf only every second weekend. Perhaps they will have to eat out twice a month instead of every week. Maybe they could vacation at Myrtle Beach or the Outer Banks every second year. Or, perhaps, they may decide to work a year or two longer and retire at 69 instead of 67. The choices will be tough.

Nancy and Steve Senior

Let's look at another working couple. Nancy and Steve Senior are both 55 years old and live in Jacksonville, Florida. Their children have graduated from college and are beginning families of their own.

Steve earns $125,000 a year as a marketing executive and plans to retire at age 66 when he will qualify for full Social Security benefits. He is covered by a 401(k) plan at work. He has contributed the maximum every year and now has $300,000 in the plan. It is all in mutual funds, 60% in stocks and 40% in corporate bonds. Steve has another $100,000 in an IRA rolled over from the profit sharing plan of a previous employer. It is invested entirely in stocks.

Nancy, an accomplished musician, earns $20,000 a year as a church choir director and organist. She earns an additional $15,000 a year by giving private music lessons in their home. She loves her work and plans to continue working for as long as she can. As she has said to the members of the choir, "They will have to carry me away from here in a box, and I will still be conducting from the grave." Nancy has been contributing $2,000 to an IRA for almost 20 years, and she has just over $81,000 in it. It is all in stock mutual funds.

Let's apply the Six Steps to Worry-Free Investing to the Seniors.

Step 1: Set Goals

Steve's goal is to retire at 66. Nancy does not want to retire—ever.

Step 2: Specify Targets

Their combined income is now $160,000. Since Nancy plans to continue working full time, they assume that they will only have to replace 70% of Steve's salary to maintain their current lifestyle. Seventy percent of $125,000 is $87,500.

Step 3: Compute Your Required No-Risk Saving Rate

Use the WFI method for computing the Matures' required saving rate:

a. First, get an estimate of their expected Social Security benefits at age 66. Using the Quick Calculator at the Social Security Administration's Web site, *www.ssa.gov/OACT/quickcalc/ calculator.html*, we find that Steve can expect $23,556 a year ($1,963 per month), and Nancy can expect $13,428 a year ($1,119 per month). The total is $36,984.

b. Subtract this from their target income of $87,500 to get $50,516 in today's dollars as the annual amount that must come from retirement saving.

c. To find out how much they need in their retirement account at age 66, we will assume a combined life expectancy of 95 years. That means they need enough for 29 years in retirement. Applying the formula for the present value of an annual amount is:

$$PV = \frac{1 - \dfrac{1}{(1+i)^n}}{i} \cdot X$$

Assuming a 3% real rate of interest or i, n is 29 years, and X is $50,516, we find the sum they need at age 66 to be about $998,404.

If we use the AnnuityNet.com calculator, the quoted price for an inflation-proof joint life annuity of $50,516 per year ($4,210 per month) is about $1,000,000. We will use this number.

The next step is to calculate how much of their salary to save each year to reach that goal. They have 11 years until Steve plans to retire. Steve already has $400,000 in his 401(k) and IRA, and Nancy has $81,000 in her IRA. Together they have a combined total of $481,000. The formula for computing the amount this will grow to by retirement is:

$$FV = PV(1+i)^n$$

Substituting $481,000 for PV, .03 for i, and 11 for n, we find that FV = $665,816. So we subtract this from the $1,000,000 needed at retirement, and that leaves $334,184.

Now we use the formula to find the annual contribution needed to reach a desired future value:

$$FV = \frac{(1+i)^{n+1} - (1+i)}{i} X$$

In this case, FV is $334,184, i is .03, and n is 11. Substituting these values into the formula, we find that the annual contribution X is $25,332. This is 15.83% of their $160,000 per year in combined salaries. This means Steve will have to contribute the maximum he is allowed under his employer's 401(k) plan, and Nancy will have to contribute as much as she can to her IRA.

Step 4: Determine Your Tolerance for Risk

The Seniors do not have much capacity for taking investment risk. Steve is 11 years away from retirement, and he does not want to work after age 66. His job as a marketing executive is likely to be sensitive to the state of the economy. If there is a prolonged economic downturn, he might find himself forced into early retirement.

Nancy's income is less likely to be affected by the state of the economy, and she plans to continue working. But she could decide to cut back after age 66, so the $35,000 they assumed she would earn might decline.

Of the $481,000 in retirement savings they now have, $120,000 (25%) is invested in Steve's 401(k) corporate bond fund, and the remaining $361,000 (75%) is in stock funds. They are taking far more risk than they should. They should move quickly to switch

their investments into TIPS or a stable value fund. The Seniors
may still want to maintain some level of participation in the
upside potential of the stock market, but we would suggest
limiting it to 10% of their assets.

Step 5: Choose Your Risky Asset Portfolio

Steve and Nancy could use the savings they accumulate outside
their retirement accounts to buy long-term call options on a
market index. As discussed earlier, buying such call options would
give them significant participation in big gains if the stock market
were to really take off. However, they will lose every penny
invested if stock prices do not rise. Alternatively, they could buy
the principal-protected equity-linked securities described in
Chapter 7.

Step 6: Minimize Taxes and Transaction Costs

The Seniors already maximize their tax advantages by using
401(k) plans, where the interest earned is not taxed. By buying
their TIPS directly from the Treasury department, when Steve
lowers risk by converting his stock funds, Steve and Nancy avoid
transaction costs.

(S) ··· (U) ··· (M) ··· (M) ··· (A) ··· (R) ··· (Y)

In this chapter, you have considered real-life cases of retirement investing that may resemble your own situation. We sum them up in Table 11.1. In all three of our examples, the same Six Steps to Worry-Free Investing apply.

Table 11.1 Summary of Our Case Studies

	Paul Younger	Mary & Marty Mature	Nancy & Steve Senior
Age	30	45	55
Annual Income	$30,000	$75,000	$160,000
Retirement Age	67	67	66 for Steve; never for Nancy
Social Security Benefits	$13,812	$30,228	$36,984
Target Income from Retirement Savings	$7,188	$22,272	$50,516
Current Retirement Fund	$9,664	$66,000	$481,000

Table 11.1   Summary of Our Case Studies (Continued)

	Paul Younger	Mary & Marty Mature	Nancy & Steve Senior
Required Saving Rate	3.85%	12.66%	15.83%
Risk Tolerance	high	moderate	low
Recommended Asset Mix	1/3 of contributions to TIPS fund; 2/3 to stock index fund	All retirement accounts in TIPS and stable value funds; outside money in stock index fund	90% in TIPS, I Bonds, and stable value; 10% at risk—maybe in options

The key to successful investment for retirement is the availability today of TIPS and I Bonds. You should build your retirement investment plan around these innovative securities in combination with your 401(k) or similar retirement plan and regular and Roth IRAs.

If you are saving more than enough to achieve your retirement target safely by investing in inflation-protected bonds, then you can invest the extra savings in the stock market. If not, you must either save more over the coming years, plan to retire later, or reduce your retirement income goals.

In the next chapter, you will consider some answers to frequently asked questions that provide a deeper look into our investment strategy toward a more worry-free investment life.

12

Frequently Asked Questions (FAQs) About Worry-Free Investing

In this chapter, you will explore:

· Aspects of investment help

· How worry-free investing differs from traditional investment strategies

· How to create your own personal finance statement

S ome of the most Frequently Asked Questions (FAQs) about worry-free investing are listed below. You explore each question in detail in this chapter.

Whom can I trust?

Is there help available from the Securities and Exchange Commission (SEC) for investors?

How do the Six Steps to Worry-Free Investing differ from the SEC's Roadmap to Saving and Investing?

Do I need to prepare a personal financial statement?

What should I do if someone gives me a hot tip about a stock or other investment?

How can I tell when stock prices are about to go up or down?

Which are the best index funds for small investors?

Should I invest in an Exchange-Traded Fund (ETF) instead of an index fund?

What is the difference between buying Treasure Inflation-Protected Securities (TIPS) and buying shares in a TIPS mutual fund?

Is a 529 plan the only way to save for a child's college education?

If I have spare cash available, am I better off using it to pay off my mortgage more quickly or investing it in some other worry-free investing asset?

Whom Can I Trust?

When it comes to investing your money, do not trust anyone completely. Never relinquish your right to decide how your money is invested, and always insist on understanding an investment that is being proposed before investing in it—what the risks are and what commissions and other expenses are involved. **If you do not understand it, don't invest in it.**

Even if your broker is your older sister, do not give her unlimited discretion over your investment accounts. Even though you are sure she has your best interests at heart, she may not make the same choices you would make. You will hold her responsible for the performance of the portfolio, and it might not do well. Many close family relationships have been spoiled in this way.

Never, ever, give anyone who makes money from commission discretion to actively manage your investments. It would be the equivalent of asking the fox to guard the hen house. Almost all investment managers make at least part of their living from commissions on sales of investment vehicles. They are professionals who see you as a customer. If they work for a firm, they are under heavy pressure from their superiors to increase earnings from commissions and other sales charges. They all believe they deserve every penny in commissions they receive. (Have you ever met anyone who thought he was *over*paid for the work he does?)

Often commissions are not transparent. For example, when you buy bonds from a securities firm, you are charged a markup over the firm's purchase cost, but it will not be called a commission. This markup is called the *bid-asked spread*. When you buy an investment from an insurance company, the price you are quoted includes a sales commission for the salesperson. Always insist on knowing how much it is.

Is There Help Available from the SEC for Investors?

The U.S. Congress created the SEC in 1934 following the stock market crash of 1929. The primary mission of the SEC is to protect investors and maintain the integrity of the securities markets. The SEC offers the public a wealth of educational information on its Internet Web site, *www.sec.gov.* The site includes the EDGAR database of disclosure documents that public companies are required to file with the commission.

The laws and rules that govern the securities industry in the United States derive from a simple and straightforward concept: All investors, whether large institutions or private individuals, should have access to certain basic facts about an investment prior to buying it. To achieve this, the SEC requires public companies to disclose meaningful financial and other information to the public, which then provides a common pool of knowledge for all investors to use to judge for themselves if a company's securities are a good investment.

The SEC also oversees other key participants in the securities world, including stock exchanges, broker dealers, investment advisors, mutual funds, and public utility holding companies. Here again, the SEC is concerned primarily with promoting disclosure of important information, enforcing the securities laws, and protecting investors who interact with these various organizations and individuals.

Crucial to the SEC's effectiveness is its enforcement authority. Each year the SEC brings between 400 and 500 civil enforcement actions against individuals and companies that break the securities laws. **Typical infractions include insider trading, accounting fraud, and providing false or misleading information about securities and the companies that issue them.**

How Do the Six Steps to Worry-Free Investing Differ from the SEC's Roadmap to Saving and Investing?

Let's look at Tables 12.1 and 12.2 to see how the approaches compare

Table 12.1   SEC's Roadmap to Saving and Investing versus Six Steps to Worry-Free Investing

SEC's Roadmap to Saving and Investing (*www.sec.gov/investor/pubs/roadmap.htm*)	Six Steps to Worry-Free Investing
Define your goals.	**1. Set goals.**
What are the things you want to save and invest for ... A home? A new car? Your education or that of a child? A comfortable retirement? The needs of your parents? All of these goals will cost money.	Make a list of the specific goals you want to achieve through your saving and investment plan, for example, "I want to continue to live at my customary standard of living after I retire," or "I want to pay for my children's college tuition at Harvard."
Make a financial plan.	**2. Specify targets.**
You'll need to figure out on paper your current situation—what you own and what you owe. You'll be creating a "net worth statement." The next step in the journey toward saving is figuring out your monthly income and expenses.	Determine the amount of money you will need to achieve each goal. These amounts become the targets of your plan.
	3. Compute your required no-risk saving rate.
	Figure out how much you need to save as a fraction of your earnings on the assumption that you take no investment risk.

Table 12.1   SEC's Roadmap to Saving and Investing versus Six Steps to Worry-Free Investing (Continued)

SEC's Roadmap to Saving and Investing (*www.sec.gov/ investor/pubs/roadmap.htm*)	Six Steps to Worry-Free Investing
Determine your risk tolerance.	**4. Determine your tolerance for risk.**
What are the best saving and investing products for you? The answer depends on when you will need the money, your goals, and if you will be able to sleep at night if you purchase a risky investment where you could lose your principal. If you are saving for retirement, and you have 35 years before you retire, you may want to invest in riskier investment products, knowing that if you stick to only th "savings" products or to less risky investment products, your money will grow too slowly—or given inflation or taxes, you may lose the purchasing power of your money. A frequent mistake people make is putting money they will not need for a very long time in investments that pay a low amount of interest. On the other hand, if you are saving for a short-term goal, you don't want to choose risky investments, because when it's time to sell, you may have to take a loss. Since investments often move up and down in value rapidly, you want to make sure that you can wait and sell at the best possible time.	Using as your benchmark the lowered-risk plan you have created in Steps 1–3, evaluate how much risk you are willing to take. The very definition of risky or safe investing will depend on the target. For most people, TIPS and I Bonds have substantially lowered risk if the goal is retirement, but for college saving, special tuition-linked accounts are safer.

Table 12.1 SEC's Roadmap to Saving and Investing versus Six Steps to Worry-Free Investing (Continued)

SEC's Roadmap to Saving and Investing (*www.sec.gov/ investor/pubs/roadmap.htm*)	Six Steps to Worry-Free Investing
Investment Products.	**5. Choose your risky asset portfolio.**

Your choices:
 	
    Stocks and bonds
    Mutual funds
 	
Because it is sometimes hard for investors to become experts on various businesses—what are the best steel, automobile, or telephone companies—investors often depend on professionals who are trained to investigate and recommend companies that are likely to succeed. Since it takes work to pick the stocks or bonds of the companies that have the best chance to do well in the future, many investors choose to invest in mutual funds.
	After deciding how much of your wealth you are willing to put at risk, choose a form for taking that risk that gives you the greatest expected gain in welfare.

	6. Minimize taxes and transaction costs.
You need to look carefully at how much a fund costs and think about how much it will cost you over the amount of time you plan to own its shares. If two funds are similar in every way except one charges a higher fee than the other, you'll make more money choosing the fund with the lower cost.	Make sure that you are not paying any more in taxes, fees, or other investment costs than is necessary.

Table 12.1   SEC's Roadmap to Saving and Investing versus Six Steps to Worry-Free Investing (Continued)

SEC's Roadmap to Saving and Investing (*www.sec.gov/investor/pubs/roadmap.htm*)	Six Steps to Worry-Free Investing
Pick a financial professional.	**Do you need professional advice?**
The best way to settle on an investment professional is to know what type of services you need and then figure out who is best suited to get the job done for you. Once you know that ask your friends and colleagues whom they recommend. Try to get several recommendations, then arrange a face-to-face meeting. Make sure you get along with the financial professional. Make sure that he or she understands your goals and risk tolerance.	Even if you agree with the ideas in this book, you may need help actually pulling the trigger to make the changes necessary to apply this new approach. If you have difficulty picking up the phone to sell your current mutual funds to buy the TIPS we suggest, you need a financial planner or an investment advisor. You may not feel comfortable going to a bank to buy TIPS or getting online to buy an inflation-indexed annuity. A financial advisor can help.
Avoid problems.	
Choosing someone to help you with your investments is one of the most important investment decisions you will ever make. While most investment professionals are honest and hardworking, you must watch out for those few unscrupulous individuals. They can make your life's savings disappear in an instant. Securities regulators and law enforcement officials can and do catch these wrongdoers. But catching them doesn't always get your money back. Too often, the money is gone. The good news is you can avoid potential problems by protecting yourself.	Your needs may be more fundamental than that. You may need help setting up a budget and sticking to it so you can achieve your goals. Consider hiring a financial planner. You may need help with setting up wills or trusts to protect your assets for your children. Get it. You may need guidance as to how much insurance and what kinds of insurance you need, other than basic house and life insurance. Seek help. Also, you may need help in remembering to revisit your plan on a regular basis to make sure you are still on target.

Table 12.2 Definitions of Saving and Investing

SEC Definitions of Saving and Investing	Worry-Free Investing Definitions of Saving and Investing
Your "savings" are usually put into the safest places or products that allow you access to your money at any time. Examples include saving accounts, checking accounts, and certificates of deposit. But there's a tradeoff for security and ready availability. Your money is paid a low wage as it works for you. Most smart investors put enough money in a savings product to cover an emergency, like sudden unemployment. Some make sure they have up to six months of their income in savings so that they know it will absolutely be there for them when they need it. When you "invest," you have a greater chance of losing your money than when you "save." Unlike FDIC-insured deposits, the money you invest in securities, mutual funds, and other similar investments are not federally insured. You could lose your "principal," which is the amount you've invested. But then, how "safe" is a savings account if you leave all your money there for a long time, and the interest it earns doesn't keep up with inflation? The answer to that question explains why many people put some of their money in savings, but look to investing so they can earn more over long periods of time, say three years or longer.	Saving means setting aside part of your current income for the future. Your savings is the cumulative amount you have saved, and investing is deciding in what form to hold your assets. For example, suppose you earn $50,000 this year and spend only $40,000 on food, clothing, transportation, rent, medical care, entertainment, and taxes. You have saved $10,000. Where did you put it? You may have left it in your checking account without making any conscious decision to do so. That is what would naturally happen if you deposit your salary into your checking account and then pay for all of your purchases by check. Even though you did not consciously choose to invest your savings in your checking account, that is what you did by default. We would say that you saved $10,000 and invested it in your checking account. Is that a good way to invest your savings? It depends. If you need liquidity, then you might consciously choose to keep your savings invested in your checking account. In general, however, it is possible to earn more while retaining most of the liquidity you need by investing in a companion savings account or a money market account.

Table 12.2   Definitions of Saving and Investing (Continued)

SEC Definitions of Saving and Investing	Worry-Free Investing Definitions of Saving and Investing
Though there are no guarantees, investing means you may earn much more money than by relying upon no-risk savings. Investors are not promised a return, but they do get the opportunity of making money that more than offsets the cost of inflation.	If you do not plan to touch your savings for at least six months, then you can certainly do better with no sacrifice of safety by investing in I Bonds. Note that investment decisions often take place without any saving taking place. An example is when you use money in your checking account to buy I Bonds. On the other hand, every time you save some income you are *implicitly* making an investment decision, because the additional saving has to be kept in some form.

Do I Need to Prepare a Personal Financial Statement?

Not really. Of course, these are helpful. But, too often people fail to take effective control of their saving and investment decisions because they get bogged down in unnecessary details. There is remarkably little data that is essential for carrying out the Six Steps to Worry-Free Investing.

To get going, all you really need to know is your current labor income—wages, salary, or income from your own business —and your major assets—savings and investment accounts, and value of your home equity. You may have a pretty good estimate of these items without even looking them up in your records. If you do not remember, you can often find the information you need in your tax returns.

So, why do financial planners generally require you to fill out forms that can take you hours or even days of preparation?

This information can be very useful. It forces you to thoroughly review aspects of your personal financial life that you may have forgotten about. You may discover old bank accounts you stuffed into a drawer years ago, or you may recall a rich uncle who died and left you some money in his will. Reviewing the details of your expenses can help you identify discretionary items to cut so that you can increase your saving.

Below we provide a standard set of personal financial statements, balance sheet, and a statement of income and expenses. **We strongly recommend that you fill these out, at least in an approximate way. But do not allow your failure to do so stand in the way of your implementing the Six Steps to Worry-Free Investing.**

Balance Sheet (Net Worth Statement)

Your net worth is the difference between your assets and your liabilities. See Tables 12.3 and 12.4 for figuring your net worth and monthly expenses.

Table 12.3   Net Worth Statement

Assets	Current Market Value	Liabilities	Amount
Cash and bank accounts		Mortgage balance	
Retirement accounts: IRAs, 401(k), etc.		Credit card debt	
Other investments including cash value of life insurance		Car loans and other loans	
Home			
Other real estate			
Value of your own business			
Art, antiques, and other personal property			
Total		**Total**	

Table 12.4   Monthly Income and Expenses

Income	
Expenses	
Housing—rent or mortgage payment	
Electricity	
Gas/oil	
Telephone	
Water/sewer	
Property tax	
Furniture	
Food	
Transportation	
Insurance	
Education	
Recreation	
Health care	
Gifts	
Other	
Total Expenses	
Income – Expenses =	

What Should I Do If Someone Gives Me a Hot Tip About a Stock or Other Investment?

In general, just listen politely and forget about it. (Unless it is a TIPS!) If an investment opportunity sounds too good to be true, it is probably far more risky than it seems. Beware of expressions such as "enormous profit potential." Remember that in the world of stocks, commodities, and real estate, there are many ways to get a shot at high profits per dollar invested, but the flip side is that you can easily lose your entire investment.

There is no harm done in investing a small amount of your money in some hot stock that a friend, neighbor, or coworker recommends, provided you treat it the same way you would a tip at the race track. Typically, there is a very small chance of big returns and a big chance of losing your entire investment.

How Can I Tell When Stock Prices Are About to Go Up or Down?

You can't. Nobody can. Just look at the wide differences in forecasts made by experts. Even when they can agree on the general direction of change, they will disagree by how much.

For example, in an article entitled "Dueling Gurus," the *New York Times* (September 2, 2001) reported that Robert Shiller and Jeremy Siegel, two professors who specialize in analyzing the stock market (Shiller at Yale and Siegel at the Wharton School) had strikingly different market forecasts. Although both have Ph.D.s in economics from the same university (MIT) and have been close friends since their graduate student days: Shiller is a "bear" and Siegel a "bull." On this day, Shiller argued that the U.S. stock market was vastly overvalued, and he predicted generally poor performance until share prices realign themselves with "fundamental" values. Siegel disagreed. Each of them represented a large group of similarly minded professional economists and market forecasters.

What Are the Best Index Funds for Small Investors?

The best index funds are the ones that perform their function at the lowest cost to their shareholders. Index fund shareholders are content with the average performance of a market. They are skeptical that an active manager can improve on performance without raising risk. Index funds delay capital gains taxes because turnover (buying and selling) is low.

A good Web site for finding descriptions of index funds and comparing their costs is *www.indexfunds.com.* If you decide to invest in stocks, we recommend picking Vanguard's Total Stock Index (VTSMX). It employs a passive management strategy designed to track the performance of the Wilshire 5000 Index, which consists of all the U.S. common stocks traded regularly on the New York Stock Exchange (NYSE), American Stock Exchange (AMEX), or Over the Counter (OTC) markets. It has the lowest expense ratio of all the funds in this category, and Vanguard is a respected company that pioneered retail index funds.

Should I Invest in an ETF Instead of an Index Fund?

An ETF is essentially a mutual fund that trades like a single stock. Until the development of the ETF, this was not possible. An ETF is a basket of stocks that reflects the composition of an index, like the S&P 500 or the Nasdaq 100. The ETF's trading value is based on the Net Asset Value (NAV) of the underlying stocks that it represents. Think of it as a mutual fund that you can buy and sell at a price that changes throughout the day.

While most mutual funds are priced at their NAV at 4:00 p.m. daily, the price of the ETF changes throughout the day. ETFs can also be bought on margin (money borrowed from your broker) and sold short. Unlike regular stocks, ETFs can also be sold short on a downtick (in a market that is moving down).

The expense ratios for most ETFs are extremely low, and they are managed so as to minimize the taxes payable by shareholders on capital gains. When traditional mutual fund investors sell all or part of their investment, all of the investors in that fund suffer capital gains tax consequences. While ETF investors may suffer capital gains costs as the result of dividend payouts or index rebalancing, they do not suffer these consequences from redemptions in the fund.

All U.S.-based ETFs currently trade on AMEX,[1] though the NYSE plans to introduce ETFs in the near future. Shares can be purchased the same way you would purchase a normal stock. Like individual stocks, ETFs have ticker symbols (like DIA or QQQ)

---

1.   *www.amex.com.*

and can be purchased through a broker. Likewise, you sell shares in an ETF the same way you would sell shares of a normal stock.

One feature of ETFs makes them distinctly different from index funds. Index funds sell and redeem shares in the fund at their NAV. While ETFs are tied to a basket of underlying stocks, the price of an ETF share can sell at a premium or a discount to its NAV. The ETF's price is kept close to its NAV by arbitrage. Traders will step in to profit from very small differences between the price and NAVs. A good Web site for finding descriptions of ETFs is *www.indexfunds.com*.

What Is the Difference Between Buying TIPS and Buying Shares in a TIPS Mutual Fund?

TIPS are issued by the U.S. Treasury, pay interest every six months, and have specific maturity dates. An investor who holds a TIPS bond to maturity is assured of receiving the face value of the bond fully adjusted for inflation. TIPS mutual funds are pools of TIPS of different maturities managed by investment companies such as Vanguard and Fidelity. Shares in the mutual funds are bought and redeemed by customers at the current NAV, which changes every day. There is no specific maturity date or promised payment for shares in the fund. Therefore, shareholders in the fund can have no assurance of the value of their shares at any time in the future. Nonetheless, over time, the performance of a TIPS fund will be closely tied to the rate of inflation and will deliver a real rate of return that is an average of the interest rates on the TIPS in the portfolio.

Here is a list of some mutual funds that invest in TIPS:

- American Century Inflation-Adjusted Bond Fund (ACTIX)
- BBH Inflation-Indexed Securities (BBHIX)
- Fidelity Inflation-Protected Bond Fund (FINPX)
- GMO Inflation-Indexed Bond Fund (GMIIX)
- PIMCO Real Return Bond Fund (PRRDX)
- Vanguard Inflation-Protected Securities (VIPSX)

One or more of these funds may be available as a choice in your employer's 401(k) plan. We recommend that you choose the one with the lowest expense ratio.

Is a 529 Plan the Only Way to Save for a Child's College Education?

The 529 plan is the most recently available and most worry-free way to invest for a child's education. In fairness, there are as many ways to save for a child's education as there are ways to invest. But only the 529 plan is likely to hedge against inflation and taxes to your maximum advantage. In some states, prepaid tuition plans may stack up favorably, though you may need an experienced financial advisor to make an accurate comparison. To give some context to the comparison, some of the other ways of going about saving for a child's college education include:

- **Coverdell Education Savings Accounts (formerly known as Educational IRAs)**—These are tax-deferred savings accounts that allow you to save up to $2,000 per year for each child under the age of 18. They are nondeductible contributions that can be made in addition to traditional IRAs or a Roth IRA. If you attempt to use money from a traditional IRA for the purpose of a college education, you will find you need to pay taxes on the amount withdrawn.

- **Growth Stocks and Growth Mutual Funds**—Yes, some people do use these to fund college educations. But as you saw in considerable detail in Chapter 6, long-term gains in stock-related investments can be risky.

- **Prepaid Tuition Plans**—With these, you can lock into the tuition price being charged at a state school in the year you enroll in the college. State officials set the amount you need to pay, and this amount depends on the targeted enrollment date and current tuition levels. The state invests the money with the intention of making its gain through its investments (riding the float). With most prepaid tuition plans, you can later transfer the funds to a private or out-of-state school, though you will have to pay the difference between the prepaid tuition amount and the current tuition of the school to which you are transferring the amount.

- **College Savings Plans**—State-sponsored investment accounts, usually with guaranteed returns, allow you to use the money at any college or university in that state. The

investment grows tax-free until the child enters college, at
which time it is taxed at the student rate.

· **CollegeSure® Certificates of Deposit (CDs)**—These CDs are
guaranteed and were discussed in Chapter 4.

· **U.S. Savings Bonds**—Using these for college funding involves
knowing a number of restrictions, although those qualifying
do not have to pay tax on the interest accrued as long as it
goes entirely for college education. The age of the parents,
amount of the family's income, and when you buy the bonds
are all factors to consider. The interest rates on these bonds
also change periodically.

· **Zero Coupon Bonds**—These are available through brokerage
houses. Like U.S. Treasury bonds they are sold at a fraction
of their eventual face value. You can get municipal and
corporate versions of these, though the Treasury versions,
sold under acronyms like STRIPS, TIGRS, and CATS, are
safer. The rub with all of these is that you have to pay taxes
on the interest as it is earned, even though you don't receive
it until the bonds mature, so you'll probably need a tax
professional to help you figure that.

· **Baccalaureate Bonds**—These are zero coupon municipal
bonds designed specifically for college savings plans. Issues of
these usually sell out quickly and are only offered
sporadically. They are exempt from federal taxes, and state
taxes, too, if you remain a resident of the state from which

you purchased them. You can find out more about these from state educational financial advisors. You may need an advisor to compute the somewhat complex investment return in relation to other investment vehicles for your tax bracket.

These are only a few of the ways to save for a child's college education. Doing your homework is the safest way to see what works best for you, but for most people, the quick, worry-free answer is a 529 plan.

If I Have Spare Cash Available, Am I Better Off Using It to Pay Off My Mortgage More Quickly or Investing It in Some Other Worry-Free Investing Asset?

The rule of thumb here is to pay off your debts early if the interest rate you are paying is greater than the interest rate you can earn by investing in a worry-free asset. This rule applies to all of your personal debts—credit card debt, auto loans, and home mortgage loans.

Applying this rule in the case of credit card debt is simple because the interest rate you are paying is prominently posted on your monthly statement. You can compare it to current bank deposit rates or money market rates that are usually displayed on your monthly bank statement. The interest rate on your credit card debt will almost always be greater, so you might as well adopt the simple rule to pay off all of your credit card debt as soon as you possibly can.

However, fixed-rate mortgage loans are a different story. In the past, long-term interest rates have fluctuated over a wide range. In the late 1970s, interest rates rose to an all-time high, and in 1979 the rate on 30-year U.S. Treasury bonds reached above 16% per year.

If you took a fixed-rate mortgage loan in the early 1970s at a rate of 6% per year, you were sitting pretty. If you had spare cash in 1979, it would have been foolish to pay off a 6% mortgage instead of investing the cash to earn 16% on 30-year bonds.

At the time of this book's writing, interest rates on fixed-rate mortgages were about 5% per year, and so was the 30-year Treasury rate. Interest rates can change, and in the future, they may rise significantly. Before you decide to pay your mortgage off early, compare the rate you are paying to the current rate on Treasury bonds. If Treasuries are paying a higher rate than you are paying on your mortgage, invest in Treasuries instead of paying off your mortgage.

Note: In deciding whether you should pay off your mortgage early, it is not enough to simply compare your mortgage rate to the rate of return you expect to earn in the stock market. Even if you believe that the expected return on stocks is higher than your mortgage rate, stocks are far riskier and you must take proper account of this extra risk.

In this chapter, you have dug a bit deeper into worry-free investing by considering some FAQs.

In the next chapter, you will find a toolbox of additional sources of information that may be useful to you as you seek to redesign your investment strategy toward a more worry-free approach.

(C) (H) (A) (P) (T) (E) (R)

13

The Worry-Free Toolbox

In this chapter, you explore:

· Web sites for more useful information

· Dealing with money when you retire

· Taking your risk inventory

Web Sites Related to Inflation-Protected Securities

n this book, you have discovered a new worry-free approach to investing that allows you to accumulate the funds you need for retirement and other lifecycle goals with far less risk than any other approach. We have tried to be clear and specific without overwhelming you with details. As you try to implement this approach, inevitably questions will arise. Fortunately, there is an abundance of useful information on the Internet to help fill in the gaps and to answer any questions we did not answer. We start off this chapter by identifying the Web sites that are most closely aligned with our approach to investing.

The Web sites we recommend to you in this chapter have two key features:

1. They do not mislead you.

2. They are free.

There are many free Web sites on investments—too many. When something of value is offered to you for free, it is natural to wonder why. There are at least two possible reasons. The first is that the sponsors want to persuade you to buy some product or service. In such cases, it is unlikely that the information and advice you receive from these sources will be unbiased. You should be very cautious and selective in using them.

The second reason for the free investment advice is that some public-spirited individual or group is trying to do a good deed. It is inexpensive to create a Web site for the posting and dissemination of advice in electronic form. As a consequence, many self-appointed gurus have taken it upon themselves to do so. Unfortunately, much of the investment advice provided at such well-intentioned sites is just as misleading as the biased commercially sponsored advice. Some of it is downright nuts. Nonetheless, with some guidance, you can avoid the bad stuff and derive much useful information from Web sites of both types.

We start with Web sites devoted to inflation-protected securities, since they are the foundation for worry-free investing.

Remember that Web sites periodically change their layouts, so it may be possible that some of these sites have changed by the time you visit them. They may even have disappeared altogether.

I Bonds

www.savingsbonds.gov/sav/sbiinvst.htm

This is the U.S. Treasury's official Web site for Series I Savings Bonds. It is very user friendly and packed with useful information. Especially useful is "Frequently Asked Questions About I Bonds" (*www.savingsbonds.gov/sav/sbifaq.htm*). You can buy I Bonds directly from this site (*www.savingsbonds.gov/ols/olshome.htm*) using your credit card, and download a Wizard (*www.savingsbonds.gov/sav/savwizar.htm*) that enables you to keep track of your bonds and update their growing value automatically each month. You can even print out handsome gift certificates for I Bonds that you purchase as gifts for others.

Treasury Inflation-Indexed Securities (TIPS)

www.publicdebt.treas.gov/sec/seciis.htm

This is the U.S. Treasury's official Web site for TIPS. It has all the information you need on how to buy TIPS either through a broker or via TreasuryDirect, and how they are treated for tax purposes. It also has a complete listing of all TIPS issued by the U.S. Treasury and the value of the Consumer Price Index (CPI) at the time they were issued.

Tax-Exempt Inflation-Protected Securities

www.cumber.com/special/mips.htm

This Web site has comprehensive information about tax-exempt municipal bonds that have inflation-linked interest payments. Although their credit risk is higher than U.S. Treasury bonds, these bonds offer investors protection against both inflation and taxes.

Inflation-Proof Annuities

client.annuitynetadvisor.com/products/individual/inflation/index.asp

This Web site is owned by AnnuityNet.com. It sells its annuities directly to customers, thus avoiding the large sales fees generally associated with annuities. The site has much useful educational material about life annuities. Most importantly, you can get price quotes for inflation-proof annuities at *client.annuitynetadvisor.com/decisions/annuity_quote.asp*.

College Tuition

www.collegeboard.com

The College Board has a great deal of information about college costs and on state 529 college savings plans. To find out more about the College Sure® Certificate of Deposit (CD), which is indexed to college costs and is guaranteed to meet future college costs, you can log on to *www.collegesavingsbank.com*.

Current Interest Rates

U.S. Treasury Yields: www.bloomberg.com/markets/ C13.html

Here you can find out the current interest rates on conventional Treasury bonds and TIPS of all maturities.

General Information for Investors

Security and Exchange Commission: www.sec.gov/ investor.shtml

The SEC's Office of Investor Education and Assistance provides a variety of useful educational materials for investors.

InvestorGuide: www.investorguide.com

InvestorHome: www.investorhome.com

Index Funds and Exchange-Traded Funds (ETFs)

IndexFunds: www.indexfunds.com/home.php

This Web site is devoted exclusively to providing unbiased information about low-cost index mutual funds and electronically traded funds. Its owner, IndexFunds, Inc., is an independent media firm and not a broker or dealer in securities. For each asset class, there are several popular indexes to choose from. Its goal is to identify the funds that track those indexes efficiently and cheaply. None of the funds on their list charge front or deferred loads, or 12b-1 fees.

Options and Long-Term Equity Anticipation Securities (LEAPS)

Chicago Board Options Exchange Online Learning Center: www.cboe.com/LearnCenter/cboeeducation/CourseList.html

At this Web site you will find excellent free online tutorials on options and LEAPS.

Taxes and Management Fees

Beginning Investor's Tax Guide: www.fairmark.com/begin

This Web site provides an introduction to tax rules all investors should know with useful links to other sources of more detailed tax information.

Personal Fund: www.personalfund.com

This Web site shows you the impact of mutual fund management fees and taxes on the returns of any mutual fund you may be considering investing in. For example, it shows that one large cap U.S. equity fund with a 10-year pretax compound annual return of 11.1% through December 31, 2001, returned only 8.5% per year on an after-tax basis and management fees. You can plug into its after-tax calculator the return on any fund to see the impact of taxes on your return.

Interactive Calculators

FinanCenter: www.financenter.com

American Savings Educational Council: www.asec.org/

These two sites have a number of online interactive calculators to help you figure out how much you will need to set aside for retirement or college, how inflation will affect your savings, and whether it is better to pay off your mortgage with your savings or leave your savings to earn interest.

Stock Research on Individual Companies

We do *not* recommend that you invest in the stocks of individual companies. But if you get a hot tip and want to investigate the stock of a single company, a good way to begin is to use a free interactive stock research Wizard. MSN's Money Central (*moneycentral.msn.com/investor/research/wizards/SRW.asp*) has one and so does Quicken (*www.quicken.com/investments/seceval/*).

Note: We do not endorse their methods for evaluating stocks.

Another useful site for more sophisticated investors is that of Standard & Poor's, *www.standardandpoors.com*. At the home page click on analytical methodology under Equity to read a useful paper about how the earnings of corporations should be calculated and valued.

Other Useful Tools and Web Sites

In this book, you have also explored a few of the more traditional investment vehicles as they contrast and compare with the inflation-protected securities that are the focus of the book. To do a bit more investigating on your own, you can visit the following Web site areas.

Bonds

One of the most useful sites for learning more about bonds, particularly government bonds, is *www.investinginbonds.com*. The Web site is maintained by the Bond Market Association and contains information about all kinds of bonds. However, by clicking on Treasuries at the top of the page, you will be taken to a page where you can focus on treasuries. At this second page, you can click to open a guide to U.S. Treasury securities that includes information about TIPS and I Bonds.

For general information about the trend of interest rates, you can go to *www.bloomberg.com*. Under Markets, click on Treasuries. That will take you to a page showing what is known as the Treasury Yield Curve. This is simply a graph of the interest rates being paid by newly issued treasuries of different maturities. Above the chart, you will find a table of the actual yields for treasuries of all maturities. Below it, you will find a table of the yields on indexed treasury securities.

Mutual Funds

Since most individuals probably should not be investing in individual stocks, the first Web site to explore is *www.morningstar.com*. Morningstar specializes in tracking, researching, and reporting on mutual funds, but its site has a great deal of information on the financial markets as well as funds. Its analysts look not only at stock funds, but also bond funds and even individual stocks. Membership at the basic level is free.

Many of the major mutual fund companies also have useful Web sites, but they will usually recommend only their own funds. If you are interested in using index funds— and you should be because of their low cost and large diversification—you should check out the Vanguard Group's site at *www.vanguard.com*. Click on Personal Investor. The site also has information on buying ETFs, which is another way to invest in index funds. The Vanguard site also had a good explanation of the various options for investing for a child's education. However, it does not discuss the use of TIPS and I Bonds.

Stocks

One place to learn more about how to understand the investment value of companies is the stock research Wizard at MSN's Money Central, *moneycentral.msn.com/investor/research/wizards/SRW.asp*.

This site not only brings you up-to-date on a company you may be interested in for investment purposes but also walks you through the investment thinking. Examining General Electric

(GE), for example, the Wizard first outlines what businesses the company is in, then compares its revenues and earnings with those of similar companies. It compares the growth rate of the company's revenues and profits with those of its rivals. The report notes that investors prefer to invest in companies that have solid and growing profit margins, and provides figures and comparisons for GE.

The site also examines the company's financial health as it relates to its peers. The research function also examines how the stock has performed, and also what might change investors' opinions of GE. In effect, the Wizard walks you through an analysis of any stock you might be interested in.

Another useful site for more sophisticated investors is that of Standard & Poor's, *www.standardandpoors.com*. At the home page click on Analytical Methodology under Equity to read a useful paper about how the earnings of corporations should be calculated and valued. To practice what you think you know about investing you can go to *stocksquest.thinkquest.org*, a site that lets you play interactive investing games.

Retirement

Besides the Worry-Free Investing (WFI) calculator available at our Web site, *www.prenhall.com/worryfree/*, you should also check out the site of the Social Security Administration, *www.ssa.gov*, where you can enter your earnings, age and planned retirement age and get an estimate of what Social Security will pay when you retire.

As noted earlier in this book, you should include Social Security payments in your retirement saving and investing planning.

Another useful site is *www.moneycentral.msn.com*. The step-by-step guide to retirement planning provides useful worksheets that allow you to calculate how much money you will need at retirement to maintain your lifestyle, and to calculate if you have enough in retirement savings to live on. The retirement section of this site is well worth exploring. It also has a free interactive online planner that includes a Monte Carlo simulation of retirement income and wealth for different asset allocations.

www.immediateannuities.com is a great source for information about annuities. You can price annuities by filling in a few boxes with your age, the amount you have to invest, and the state in which you live.

Taxes and Management Fees

Another Web site is *www.personalfund.com*. It can show you the impact of mutual fund management fees and taxes on the returns of any mutual fund you may have invested in, or may be considering investing in.

You should also check out the beginning investor's tax guide at *www.fairmark.com/begin* for an introduction to tax rules all investors should know.

Investment Glossary

Finally, if you are uncertain of the meaning of any word we have used, or any word you read on any of the Web sites we have identified in this book, you will find help at *www.investorwords.com*. This online dictionary can help you understand any of the technical words you may run into while investing or researching. Simply type in the word, and the site provides a definition.

Dealing With Money When You Retire

You have just retired. You contacted the Social Security Administration three months ago to apply for your Social Security benefits, so you should be receiving your first Social Security check in the mail. You rolled your 401(k) balance into an Individual Retirement Account (IRA) from your employer's plan, and you have invested the money in TIPS, as we have argued in this book, or perhaps an inflation-protected annuity. Your spouse has done the same. You are set for life, unless you overspend your planned retirement budget.

Once you have taken virtually all the risk out of your investment portfolio by using TIPS, your main danger comes from overspending. You must budget your daily and weekly expenses to match the income generated from your retirement accounts.

If you followed the common advice, you based your income needs in retirement on 70% of your preretirement income. Now, before you are too far along in retirement, you should draw up a budget that matches your spending to your retirement income. Besides taxes, which still have to be paid, and your day-to-day living expenses, you are likely to have increasing medical expenses over time. Though you have Medicare coverage, you should buy a medigap insurance policy, plus you should consider buying a long-term care policy, if you do not already have one. After all that, you will have to budget for out-of-pocket medical expenses that aren't covered by Medicare or your medigap policy. Then you will probably want money for travel, at least in the first few years of retirement, and for leisure activities, such as golf, tennis, fishing, going to the theater. You have more time for these activities now, but they cost money.

Routine Budget Review

Review your budget each month to see how you are doing. At the end of the first year, take a good hard look at what you have spent. If you have overspent your budget, you will have to cut back, perhaps eat out, play golf, or go to the movies less often. Perhaps you have underspent your income. That's great. You can increase your spending in future years, build a cushion for emergencies, or put the money to work in investments. Since this is extra money, you could, if you wish, invest it in the stock market in the hope of increasing your nest egg. Because it is extra, you will suffer no harm to your living standard if you should lose all or part of it. If you are successful, you may be able to permanently raise your retirement standard of living or leave a bigger estate to your heirs.

If you decide to invest in stocks, we suggest using index funds because of their low costs and tax efficiency. As mentioned in earlier chapters, it is very difficult even for investment professionals to consistently earn higher returns than the market indexes, in part because of the costs of trading securities. Very few stock mutual funds beat the indexes consistently over period of even 10 years. It's equally hard to pick which of the thousands of stock mutual funds is going to be one of those that will beat the indexes in the future. When you buy an index fund, you invest in a fund that is built to exactly match the performance of the stock market as a whole. It does very little buying and selling of stocks, so it has very low trading costs, and in rising markets it generates below average capital gains tax obligations.

An index fund will give you exactly the return of the market as a whole, minus the very small management fee. If the market goes up, your retirement nest egg will grow. If it falls, you will lose some of the money you have in the index fund, but since it's extra money, your planned living standard will not suffer. Remember, though, you should not invest your core retirement assets, those needed to lock in at least your minimum acceptable standard of living, in stocks.

In fact, **it's probably best to not invest in stocks even the additional assets required to maintain your preretirement living standard. Only assets beyond these—**

what you can afford to lose—should be exposed to stock market risk.

Whatever you do, you must be careful with your money when you retire because it's difficult, if not impossible, to replace. For a few years, you may be able to work part time to replace lost income, but as you get older that will become less and less of an option. That's why you should invest only excess assets in stocks. You shouldn't take any risk with your retirement savings at any stage, but most certainly after retirement.

Taking Your Risk Inventory

Much of this book has been about self-awareness. Everyday, thousands of people invest their money thinking they can trust an outcome that is predictable when it is not.

People compete for investment returns in a casual way against seasoned professionals to whom returns mean survival. We have tried to provide paths that include more guaranteed hedges against inflation—a more worry-free path.

By reading this book, you have shown a willingness to learn more about being your own advisor or presenting a clearer picture of your needs to a financial counselor. Yet, do you really know this financial side of yourself as much as you would like? Are you fully aware of psychological aspects of yourself that could affect your investing?

Before deciding how to invest, you should make an inventory of your existing risk exposures. First of all, look at your career risk—the risk of losing your job. How stable is the income from your career? Once again, a tenured professor at a university has very little career risk. A doctor at a major hospital, or partner lawyer with major law firm, has little career risk (and both have substantial human capital during much of their careers). Public employees, protected by civil service rules and often union contracts, have relatively little career risk. However, most people employed in the private sector have some career risk. The possible loss of income from being unemployed at some stage must be considered when deciding how much and where to invest.

What about the possible loss of earnings because of illness or becoming disabled? Everyone is exposed to that risk, but it can and should be insured against using health and long-term disability insurance. There is the risk you may die before you have accumulated sufficient financial assets to provide for your family or to retire. That, too, can and should be insured against. There is the risk your house, a major asset, or your car, could be damaged by fire or flood, or some other natural disaster. These, too, can and should be insured against. There is liability risk, the risk that someone will sue you because they have suffered a loss for which you may be held responsible. For example, what if someone trips and falls and is seriously hurt while in your house. You may be held responsible. Or perhaps you are involved in a car accident in which someone is hurt. You may be held responsible. You can and should insure against those risks.

Then there is financial-asset risk—the risk you take when you
invest in stocks, bonds, etc. Once you have completed your risk
inventory, you should insure against those risks for which insurance is available, to the limit that this is reasonable and affordable. It is possible to spend too much on insurance (more than
the investments return), and if you have doubts about finding the
happy balance, you may wish to seek advice. Then your investment decisions should be made with allowance for the remaining
risk exposures.

RISK INVENTORY WORKSHEET

Table 13.1 provides a short worksheet you can use to get a quick
sense of your own risk ratio. You could also visit any of the available
more detailed Internet versions for a better understanding of your
own risk level in order to be as cautious as possible, and hence, as
worry-free as possible.

Table 13.1   Risk Inventory Worksheet

	High	Moderate	Low
Transferability of job skills (high = low risk)			
Correlation of job to the economy (high = high risk)			
Correlation of job to stock market (high = high risk)			

RISK INVENTORY WORKSHEET (CONTINUED)

Age risk (20–35 = low,
36–50 = moderate, 51+ = high)

Health risk (if fully insured,
check low)

Real asset risk, e.g., house, car
(highly insured = low risk)

Liability risk (highly insured =
low risk)

For each check in low box, add 1 point.
For each check in moderate box, add 10 points.
For each check in high box, add 20 points.

**A total score over 40 suggests
high investment risk.**

There are books[1] on this subject. There are also more detailed risk
tolerance questionnaires[2] available on the Internet that can assist
you in doing some objective personal finance profiling of yourself.
The principle advantage of responding to a risk tolerance questionnaire is as old as Socrates: "Know thyself." Think it's easy?

---

1. John Nofsinger's *The Psychology of Investing* (Upper Saddle River, NJ: Prentice Hall PTR,
2002) is a good one.
2. ProQuest (*www.ProQuest.com*) has devised a good one in conjunction with the University of New South Wales.

Chapter 13
The Worry-Free Toolbox

Most people are much mistaken about their own risk tolerance. Not that you might be a secret gambler—it's just that the recent ups and downs of the stock market alone indicate a gamesmanship sense about investing that is dangerous. Investors who remain uninformed and unadvised can become their own worst enemy.

So, how do you learn more about your own characteristics that will allow you to maximize the balance of risk versus worry? Going to the questionnaires is a good place to start. If necessary, have a spouse help with identifying your risk attributes—they probably know you better than you think. Questionnaire questions range from such fine lines as: "If you had to choose between job security with a small pay raise and less security with a big pay raise, which would you choose?" or, "How easily do you adapt when things go wrong financially?"

We suggest that every reader take some form of financial self-examination test or questionnaire. This is a lot more than a fun exercise; it can be vital if you wish to avoid financial worries later. You might well discover the one unexplored aspect of yourself that you most need to be aware of to avoid financial problems later in life.

This chapter has been something of a toolbox of resources as you assume more responsibility for understanding and taking control of your financial destiny in as worry-free a way as possible. You explored dealing with money when you retire, a few useful Web sites, and even considered a brief inventory of your own risk tolerance.

Remember, part of being worry-free is being aware, is being flexible as needed, and is revisiting your financial plans on a routine basis as the laws and financial vehicles change. This book has been your first step. Good luck in your own planning toward safe and worry-free investing.

M

Management fees and expenses, 55, 216

Market-Index Target Term Securities (MITTS), 119

Mathematical formulas
investments, computing amount needed for, 28–29, 32
retirement savings, computing amount needed for, 39

Maturity date for TIPS, 26

Medical coverage and retirement, 223

Merton, Robert C., 130

Money Central, 217, 219–20, 221

Monthly income and expenses statement, 199

Morningstar, 219

Mutual funds
loads, 55
management expenses, 55
redemption fees, 55
retirement savings and, 55
transaction costs for, 55
Web sites, 219

Myths about investing
an age-based portfolio strategy is best way to secure your lifecycle savings targets,

133–34
beating the market, 126–28
dollar cost averaging improves your risk-reward tradeoff, 132–33
inflation, stocks are best hedge against, 131–32
overview, 125–26
professionals, it is easy to beat stock market, 126–28
stocks are not risky in long run, 130
track records of money managers indicate who is best, 128–30

N

Net Asset Value (NAV), 202–3

New York Stock Exchange (NYSE), 86, 201

Nikkei crash, 103

No-risk savings rate, computing, 12, 145–46

O

Options, 216

Outliving your resources, 48–52

Overspending and retirement, 222

Z

The *Financial Times* delivers a world of business news.

Use the Risk-Free Trial Voucher below!

To stay ahead in today's business world you need to be well-informed on a daily basis. And not just on the national level. You need a news source that closely monitors the entire world of business, and then delivers it in a concise, quick-read format.

With the *Financial Times* you get the major stories from every region of the world. Reports found nowhere else. You get business, management, politics, economics, technology and more.

Now you can try the *Financial Times* for 4 weeks, absolutely risk free. And better yet, if you wish to continue receiving the *Financial Times* you'll get great savings off the regular subscription rate. Just use the voucher below.

4 Week Risk-Free Trial Voucher

Yes! Please send me the *Financial Times* for 4 weeks (Monday through Saturday) Risk-Free, and details of special subscription rates in my country.

Name _____

Company _____

Address _____ ❏ Business or ❏ Home Address

Apt./Suite/Floor _____ City _____ State/Province_____

Zip/Postal Code_____ Country _____

Phone (optional) _____ E-mail (optional)_____

Limited time offer good for new subscribers in FT delivery areas only.

To order contact Financial Times Customer Service in your area (mention offer SAB01A).

The Americas: Tel 800-628-8088 Fax 845-566-8220 E-mail: uscirculation@ft.com

Europe: Tel 44 20 7873 4200 Fax 44 20 7873 3428 E-mail: fte.subs@ft.com

Japan: Tel 0120 341-468 Fax 0120 593-146 E-mail: circulation.fttokyo@ft.com

Korea: E-mail: sungho.yang@ft.com

S.E. Asia: Tel 852 2905 5555 Fax 852 2905 5590 E-mail: subseasia@ft.com

FT FINANCIAL TIMES
World business newspaper

www.ft.com

Where to find tomorrow's best business and technology ideas. TODAY.

- Ideas for defining tomorrow's competitive strategies — and executing them.

- Ideas that reflect a profound understanding of today's global business realities.

- Ideas that will help you achieve unprecedented customer and enterprise value.

- Ideas that illuminate the powerful new connections between business and technology.

ONE PUBLISHER.
Financial Times Prentice Hall.

 **FT** Prentice Hall
FINANCIAL TIMES

WORLD BUSINESS PUBLISHER

AND 3 GREAT WEB SITES:

Business-minds.com

Where the thought leaders of the business world gather to share key ideas, techniques, resources — and inspiration.

InformIt.com

Your link to today's top business and technology experts: new content, practical solutions, and the world's best online training.

ft-ph.com

Fast access to all Financial Times Prentice Hall business books currently available.